THE REFORMATION: A PROBLEM FOR TODAY

THE
REFORMATION
A PROBLEM FOR TODAY

by Joseph Lortz

Translated by John C. Dwyer, S.J.

THE NEWMAN PRESS
WESTMINSTER, MARYLAND
1964

This translation was made from *Die Reformation als religiöses Anliegen heute* published by Paulinus Verlag, Trier, Germany

Imprimi potest: JOHN J. MCGINTY, S.J.
Provincial of the Province of New York
May 27, 1963

Nihil Obstat: JOHN A. GOODWINE, J.C.D.
Censor Librorum

Imprimatur: FRANCIS CARDINAL SPELLMAN
Archbishop of New York
September 13, 1964

Contents

THE REFORMATION: A PROBLEM FOR TODAY

Introduction

After the First World War the lecture craze came upon us with full force, and something similar is happening again in our times. It is not my intention to lecture to you, my readers, but to encourage reflection with the purpose of fostering responsible thinking for yourselves. For, although culture in the true sense cannot be too highly esteemed—and with my background in scholarly research, I certainly am not in a position to find fault with the pursuit of knowledge—still we must realize that superficial culture is something we most certainly can do without today. Our concerns must concentrate at present on the fundamental issues.

There is always difficulty in speaking to another human person and truly reaching him. It is still more difficult to make vital contact with individuals who are strangers. Furthermore, when man's most precious possession, his religion, is the topic, and when the religious beliefs involved have been centers of controversy for centuries, the difficulties are almost insurmountable. This is the situation among the Christian Churches today.

Intelligent dialog is intimately bound up with the concrete circumstances in the lives of the participants. Unfor-

tunately this fact has been lost sight of by the authors of a
number of influential manuals of philosophy and theology,
for they seem to feel that the abstract presentation of truth
in formulas that were successful in the thirteenth century
will be equally successful today.

The more delicate a situation is, the more important
it is to maintain close and intimate contact with it in all
its concrete aspects. From this it is clear that fruitful dialog in the religious sphere can come about only if we take
into account all the presuppositions implicit in a situation.
The success of any dialog is closely linked to its extremely
complex set of conditions and factors, whose very existence
may go unnoticed. Our situation today is most involved; it
offers a variety of problems for solution, problems inherited
from the confusion of the past decades that were neither
faced nor solved at that time.

Admittedly we are subject to many pressures, even external ones, so that it is consequently not always possible to
be utterly frank in our discussions. This attitude can affect
dialog to such an extent that the very possibility of engaging
in worthwhile dialog may be questionable.

Today we live at a time when many ties with the past
have been broken. Not a day passes without an awareness
of something else which has irrevocably melted into a by-
gone era. The whole framework of society has been utterly
destroyed and every attempt to remedy the situation runs
the danger of compounding the confusion. The greatest
danger of all consists in a tendency to diagnose the ills
afflicting society in our day by a superficial examination
of the symptoms; we have to get to the heart of the matter.

Here we meet another difficulty: people are just too exhausted for this task. Yet it is an inspiring experience to
meet young people in these times, students generally, who

seem willing to attack the almost innumerable problems of our age with untiring energy and genuine optimism, tempered with a sober sense of reality; to shoulder the tremendous burden of fashioning a new world from the ruins that surround us. But with the exception of these students, most would subscribe to the words addressed by Vercors to the Americans: "We are well aware of the crisis of our times; we know that we stand on the edge of the abyss; we have heard about it hundreds of times and have said it on innumerable occasions ourselves. All of us hear of it, all of us know it, but no one makes any effort to bring about a change in himself or others."

Today the preaching of the Word is needed in a more profound sense than ever before; today, because of the convulsions that have rocked the spirit of man to its foundations, it can offer an antidote to the exhaustion we have mentioned—provided only that one caution is observed: people must learn how to listen in the true sense of the word; they must once more be taught to be receptive. This caution touches on one of the major faults of our day; newspapers, radios, pamphlets, and speeches assail us from every side; we are fed up with words. The sickness in modern society is intimately linked up with the multiplication of the mass media of communication that have had such far-reaching effects on the course of history, as both a cause and a symptom of that vast superficiality to which the search for profound and genuine meaning has been sacrificed. The welter of words, in which we are incessantly immersed, is a clear expression and a most important cause of this sacrifice.

The Christian philosopher of history is consoled by the thought that when there is question of posing fundamental problems in accurate formulas, the basic concepts used are always those of a perennial Christian tradition. This is evident when we approach the problem of teaching modern man how to be receptive, to really listen; we can succeed only if we return to the fundamental Christian ideals at the very outset. When, for example, the question of guilt is raised in any discussion today, the air can be cleared and fruitful results achieved only if each begins by confessing his own guilt, if all together humbly proclaim *mea culpa*. This is true not only with regard to guilt for the last few decades or for the last war; all of us, Catholics and Protestants alike, must humbly evaluate ourselves and those with whom we live in a spirit of deep mutual responsibility in an assessment that reaches back several centuries into the past.

Still another caution is to be observed if our dialog is to be productive of results. We must approach others with respect and avoid at all costs any useless and pedantic attempt to "educate" others that is all too common in matters of this kind. No matter how radical the appeal we make, we must respect the freedom of those to whom we speak. Our Lord gave us excellent example in this matter: He spoke with authority; yet, up to that final meeting with Judas in the Garden of Gethsemane, His words never indicate that he made the slightest attempt to dominate the will of the person he was dealing with. No matter how forceful the demands we make on others, the distinctive quality of these demands must be the charity with which they are made.

Here we have another indication of the way one might succeed in making fruitful contact with the mind of others: we must stop regarding things as mere means; we must acquire the ability to honestly take things as they are, in themselves, and in their complex relationships. Those responsible for the betrayal of the past recent years approached everything with one question in mind: "What can we get out of it and how soon?" Today when certain practical and all too pragmatic individuals in our midst approach the necessary tasks of reconstruction with the same attitude, they do nothing but prove their kinship with the spirit of the Nazi regime, no matter how loud their protestations of the opposite. They represent an objectively corrosive factor. After all, how many of them dared to oppose the regime directly either in word or in deed during those years? Fortunately for them, it makes little difference today, but actually they were quite close to the spirit of that regime.

Superficial thought and action according to the formula "what can I get out of it?" and the tendency to act on mere appearances must be rejected. We must strive to get to the heart of the matter and be willing to serve. Blessed are the pure of heart! Modern man must regain a feeling for the mystery of patient and unselfish growth, a mystery expressed in the words of our Lord concerning the seed that must first die. We have to build on deeper foundations of intellectual honesty so that the superstructure will be strong and vital. We must learn how to serve. We must understand that for a long time to come, we may sow the seed, but others will reap the harvest. We will not live to see a reconstruction of the West.

The discussions that we shall undertake now will attempt to find a solution of the present crisis from an historical approach.

It is a normal temptation for a man to look for the causes of his suffering and other misfortunes of life in the mistakes, failures, and injustices that he has experienced or suffered, especially if he feels that the blame can be laid at another's door. Thus the majority of men today find the explanation for their present misfortunes in the events of the years 1933 to 1945.

Without a doubt these years do present a picture of surpassing criminal guilt, a mass betrayal without any historical parallel. But to begin our analysis basically or even exclusively with the year 1933 would be to condemn this analysis to a superficiality which we already have condemned. Analyses of today that make use of this approach and more or less timidly indicate the underlying essential character of the misfortunes tend thereby to confuse immediate causality with an historical cause in the broadest sense of the word; in other words, with the complex factors that make an event of particularly revolutionary character possible. We shall return to this point at a later stage in our study.

We must be clear on one point: we would be in serious, even mortal, danger if we were to believe that the sickness affecting Western Civilization could be cured merely by avoiding the mistakes of the recent past. It seems that the main theme of many of the articles and speeches we read today is the rejection of authoritarian rule and the freedom of the human person. This is fine, even indispensable. But merely to fight repression, merely to speak of freedom would be to limit oneself to the superficial and to preclude a solid approach to any solution. Such action is nothing more than an acceptance of that liberalism in the philosophic sense of the word, whose subjective tenets have been responsible for the arbitrary forms of government of which we have seen so much in recent years.

Another point deserves special emphasis. There is question here not only of subjective and personal values but, above all, of the objective facts of the real order. The

German people have special need to understand this; its realization must guide their thinking.

History is a record of the past; yet it does not include all the elements of the past, but those alone that influence the contemporary scene. Other elements of the past are nothing more than collectors' items. Since history is the past insofar as it influences the present scene, history is incomplete in itself; it can achieve completeness only through our own activity. This can happen in two ways. Our contribution may be a further development of the forces released by the past: we elaborate the approaches that were hinted at, the programs that were proposed, the possibilities that were vividly presented in one or more instances. At other times our contribution is more negative: to us, historical solutions appear patently insufficient and nothing more than a useless burden on the shoulders of humanity.

Both of these aspects are realized in our reaction to the Reformation. The powerful forces then unleashed and the strong personalities who wielded them have a tremendous influence on our own day. The world-wide effects of the Reformation would have to be taken into account to demonstrate this more fully. On the other hand, the Reformation is still an incomplete event. It is, to this day, a solution which has been essentially unsuccessful. Without taking into account other aspects, we have uniform agreement on at least one point: the Reformation envisaged a reform in head and members of a single Church common to all Christendom. This goal was not achieved; on the contrary, both the Church and Christianity split apart. The conclusion is quite clear: the Reformation failed in its primary objective.

We may ask whether, by a fresh and more profound interpretation of the Reformation, by a more exact under-

standing of the historical and personal problems of the time
and the real concerns of the reformers, it is possible to re-
capture again the aim of the Reformation and to offer a
better solution to its problems or at least to point the way
towards such a solution. This question I shall attempt to
answer.

In my opinion, the task of conceiving anew the goal
of the Reformation and of presenting a new solution is
of vital importance for mankind today. The proof of this
is not difficult. The so-called Christian West actually has
been dechristianized for a long period. We live in fact in
an apostate West. Where religious statistics from the large
cities are available, the figures are shocking. Ordinarily,
we are simply blind to the facts. In this respect, even the
appointed guardians of religious life, the pastors of Catholic parishes in the country, form no exception. We are
lamentably unaware of the appalling extent to which modern life has been dechristianized at its very core, for the
Christian ideal has ceased to influence those aspects of
public and private life which stem from our Christian past.
This is precisely the situation we find immediately before
the Reformation. Today in Europe and America there is
simply no such thing as Christian public life. Nowhere in
the world of politics or jurisprudence can we find anything
worthy of the name Christian except in its merely external
trappings. It would be difficult to name one major city
where this state of affairs does not obtain. It is small consolation that in the cities our churches are open and that,
on occasion, public processions take place; these do little
to alter the picture of thoroughgoing secularization. Perhaps one might attempt to relieve the otherwise black picture by noting the truly inspiring phenomena of the World
Eucharistic Congresses. But actually, a look at the numbers

involved merely makes us painfully aware of the fact that these manifestations constitute a pitifully small exception to the general rule. In Leipzig before the war, figures show that the number of those who professed membership in one of the Christian Churches lay somewhere between one and one half and two percent; this is cogent proof of the fact that Christian Europe is by no means Christian any longer.

Yet Western Civilization came into being at the moment the West became Christian. By this I mean that Christianity was not introduced into Western Civilization. At the time of the profound upheavals created in every area of ancient life by the migration of the Germanic tribes, Christianity in the form of the Latin Church and the new Germanic peoples united to form the complex structure we know as Western Civilization. In a thoroughgoing process of interpenetration, these two forces united to form a new entity: Medieval Christian Civilization. Christianity and the Germanic peoples joined in this act of a new creation and grew together in a long and complex process of life which in a most distinctive manner manifests the characteristics of a true intermingling of ideas and ideals. Their union is distinctive in that its elements can no longer be separated without destroying the composite.

The conclusion is quite obvious. Since Western Civilization is essentially Christian, it must either regain its vital contact with its Christian sources, become rechristianized, or perish. The question of the truth of Christianity is irrelevant here; the fact is that the fate of Western Civilization is bound to that of Christianity. No organism can survive unless it receives the proper kind of nourishment. The extent to which a given historical structure can change has always been limited by the constitutive elements of that structure; where the fundamental laws of any historical reality have been tampered with, collapse is soon to follow. Rodin expressed it quite well, "We barbarians were civilized by the faith and through our loss of faith we have once more become barbarians." [1] Through loss of faith, the essential, vital principle in Western Civilization has been destroyed.

No matter how many factors responsible for the de-christianization of Europe we might choose to mention, no single cause is as important as the Reformation to the extent that it led to the division of Christianity. The Reformation was not merely a divisive movement; it was much more, but essentially it was a division. Even Protestants have come more and more to this realization.

Because of this division in Christianity, the preaching of the Christian message has lost much of its convincing power. This division is in large measure responsible for the loss of the feeling for truth on the part of modern men. The attempt to preach Christianity in large cities or mission lands meets with the question: "What brand of Christianity are you preaching, Catholic or Protestant?" If Protestant, the further question arises, "What Church or sect?" Christians of all faiths, even Catholics, are aware, or more significantly unaware, of the crippling and dangerous effect of indifferentism which is a direct result of the division brought about by the Reformation.

Consequently, the union of Christian Churches is an absolutely indispensable condition for the necessary re-christianization of the West; therefore, steps must be taken to bring about that union. My own ideas on how this may be accomplished will be more fully treated later on, but one thing should be clearly understood at the very beginning: We have no desire—in fact it would be impossible

[1] Quoted by K. Weiss in *Geschichtliches Gethsemane*, p. 187.

and inexcusable—to approach the matter pragmatically; this is not a problem to be solved by some sort of busy hustling. We can have no faith in snap solutions. My earlier warnings against superficial thought and action must naturally be applied here. We want to get to the heart of the matter. To do so we must be as strict in the demands we make on ourselves as in those we make on others.

If we ask in what spirit we are to approach the task at hand, it is immediately clear that a predominantly polemic treatment must be avoided at all costs. Nothing prevents us as Catholics from regarding the Reformation as an event of the greatest importance or seeing its positive elements clearly and stating them with vigor. A necessary postulate here is the ability to think synthetically, that is, to embrace in our thinking opposite points of view and mutually opposing forces. What is needed is a breadth of view that can see life in all its complexity, in other words, an ability to see the other side of the question. We have to view the problems that arise dispassionately, with true liberty of spirit, but without manufacturing a painstaking and pedantic pseudosynthesis. This is the only way something as truly vital as history can be adequately understood, for life is essentially a dialectic of mutually opposing forces. The real is never one-sided, it always has many facets. I can speak of it truly only if I have examined all its aspects. Admittedly this can at times demand courage, but after all who is more fitted for the task than the Christian whose freedom was won for him by the Lord. When a man speaks out in a spirit of courageous freedom, his words will have unsuspected and fruitful results that are most rewarding even if they lead him to make painful admissions and acknowledge difficult obligations.

These words are addressed to both Catholics and Protestants. For centuries both groups have held unsatisfactory views of the Reformation; both groups have tended merely to justify their own positions; both have been correct on some points and completely erroneous on others.

Our approach to the facts must undergo a radical change, for once again we are face to face with a fundamental category of Christian life—*metanoia*. This means, first of all, a change in our thinking, not primarily the acquisition of any single new position or fact but of a new way of thinking. Yet nothing is more difficult to acquire than a new way of viewing a problem. *Metanoia* also means penance and this is applicable because a new approach to rethinking a question cannot remain on an abstract, theoretical level but must pass to the sphere of our daily life and be realized there. This is the sense in which both Catholics and Protestants must radically alter their approach.

Real decisions must be made and our courage must be commensurate to the task at hand. To make a decision is a painful experience because it demands that we tear ourselves away from something to which we are attached. It may happen, for example, that many Protestants will enthusiastically agree with our later discussions on the general causes of the Reformation, but will be disillusioned by the critically important statements that have to be made about Luther himself. But disillusionment is not a category to which we can cling in the face of truth.

We must be strictly and utterly honest with ourselves; we must understand and put our understanding to work. There is no question here of debate and rebuttal, collegiate-style. The principle that must guide our entire undertaking is to recognize in all history the *opus Dei,* the action of God, not theoretically or merely on the verbal level, but in reality and truth.

If we make this attempt to see the problems as they really are and if in the process Catholics and Protestants begin to approach one another in an understanding of the Reformation, the unenlightened observer might conclude that doctrinal differences were no longer too important. Nothing could be farther from the spirit and the actual conclusions of this study. Indifferentism is the deadly enemy of truth, and we want no part of it. Of course, we admit that the essence of history is complexity that may embrace conflicting elements to say nothing of contradictions. This complexity is simply an element of history with which we are faced; but to depict it honestly, even if it seems damaging to one's own position, does not require that one regard all these elements as equally true or justified.

Furthermore, a firm foundation is necessary if our assessment of historical fact is not to remain hopelessly in the clouds. As will be clear, this is of particular importance when Revelation is concerned. For the heart of Christianity is dogma, truth which can be known and clearly stated. Not that dogmatic formulas contain the fullness of divine truth, but we certainly reject that short-sighted tendency of certain philosophical liberals to despise dogma as nothing but a pitifully narrow and restrictive formula. Dogma is a guarantee of Christian truth in a form accessible to the human intellect. Dogma is the guardian of the truths of salvation, and what a man thinks of dogma depends on what that man thinks of salvation.

In other words, when we aim at furthering mutual understanding and seek to contribute to an eventual *rapprochement* of the Churches, we must start not with tolerance in matters of dogma, but with intolerance. Tolerance in matters of dogma makes the search for truth impossible.

As a Catholic and a priest, I speak with the conviction

that only the Catholic faith fully expresses Christian truth, and in the same way, the Protestant with whom I speak must be equally convinced of the fact that only his faith corresponds to the fullness of Christian truth. Only if a man is fully convinced of the truth of what he believes, can he order his life by faith. Then alone can the question of truth be properly posed, for truth is a supreme value whose demands are inexorable. There is no danger that firmness in matters of dogma will be confused with narrow-mindedness or with an ill-timed zeal aimed at conversion. Nor is there danger that our approach will be devoid of charity. It is true that in the past charity was often lacking, and it would be an exaggeration to say that Christian charity sufficiently unites us today. Mutual charity, however, in our One Lord according to the precepts of the Gospel must grow and grow. We can never be satisfied with our progress in mutual love, but it must be a love with reverence for the truth and not in spite of the truth. For truth does not oppose freedom and breadth of view but thrives in an atmosphere where both prevail. A little while ago I noted the great charity that characterized the words of our Lord; nevertheless, we must remember that He also said, "I am the truth," "The truth will make you free."

Bishop Stählin, a Lutheran, has formulated this basic attitude in a most convincing fashion: "It is not permissible to fight for anything but the truth and fullness of the Gospel and for the purity and unity of the one, holy, universal, and apostolic Church." There is no room left for a shortsighted, contentious spirit. Our responsibilities to one another are too great; thus charity must inspire every word we utter. We cannot allow this charity to be lessened by our superiority complexes.

The intolerance which we must have in matters of

dogma makes this quite difficult, for we must approach the
dialog with the firm conviction that "My form of Christianity is the right one, not yours." This indicates that there
is another prerequisite for the dialog: in our own possession
of the truth and in the missionary activity of the Church
Unity Movement we must in all humility regard ourselves
merely as tools of divine grace, or better, as indentured and
unprofitable servants. As such we don't speak for ourselves
—in good time it will be given to us to speak if our spirit of
service is genuine.

This points out once more that Christians who are separated in matters of faith must strive as never before to
realize a spirit of mutual charity. Above all, we Catholics
must realize that our own living of the truth is frequently
deficient in vitality, charity, and faith. *Metanoeite.* Love
one another. Give generously of yourselves. This does not
mean: "Be right!" We have much to learn about what it
really means to be a Christian. We must lead our Protestant
brethren into the Church and this is possible only in a spirit
of profound and unselfish charity.

The objective possibility of this basic attitude is founded
on the fact that, although dogma is inviolable and clearly
determined truth, still this truth is and must always be a
vital thing—it can never be reduced to a dead letter. This
is clear from the immense variety which Christianity as-
sumes within the framework of the Church. The genuinely
distinct character of Petrine, Pauline, and Johannine Christianity is manifest even today in the framework of their
continued, organic development.

St. Paul, inspired as he was with the spirit of the Lord,
is a magnificent example of the difficult synthesis of unyielding intolerance in matters of dogma and an all-em-
bracing love with Christian freedom. Paul devoted his

life to the struggle against the Judaizing elements within
Christianity and did not hesitate to oppose Peter openly in
this matter. Yet he is most tactful and serious in urging the
Romans to try to understand those who still hold to the
ceremonial prescriptions of the Law. He forbids the Romans to judge them adversely for it: "But him who is weak
in faith, receive, without dispute about opinions" (Romans
14:1). As long as a man acts without self-righteousness and
without striving merely to please himself (Romans 15:1b),
and as long as all his actions are in and for the Lord (Romans 14:6, 9, 13), he cannot go far wrong. Again, in Romans 14:19: "Let us, then, follow after the things that
make for peace and let us safeguard the things that make
for mutual edification." The people Paul was addressing
knew, as we know today, that peace in the Kingdom of God
has nothing to do with a weak-kneed spirit of compromise.
We must never lose sight of the words of our Lord: "I
have not come to bring peace but the sword."

Never since 1517 have prospects for such a dialog between the Churches been better than they are today. This
is due partly to developments in the area of historical
scholarship, partly to developments in the strictly religious
field. Because of the work of the last forty years, we have
a more adequate knowledge of a world that saw the end
of the Middle Ages and the early years of Luther. This has
helped to correct erroneous presentations of the late medieval period as well as the development of the "Luther legend" among the latter's contemporaries and succeeding generations. The research of Catholic scholars such as Paulus,
Denifle, Merkle, and Grisar, together with those of the
Protestant historian Otto Schell, have contributed significantly to the collapse of the Luther legend.

Religious factors, however, were even more important.

Today the very existence of the Churches is threatened. Lest I be misunderstood, let me note that by "today" I mean the situation after the Second World War, as Western Civilization stands on the brink of destruction and finds itself threatened more seriously than ever by the massive, monolithic, anti-Christian powers of the world. Of course, in the case of Germany, we cannot overlook the common experiences of the Churches under the Nazi regime. Without doubt, in innumerable cases, real Christian love and genuine commitment to Christian Faith manifested their integrity and vitality so profoundly in the time of persecution that they became a powerful force of growth toward union. Above all the martyrs and confessors of both Churches in the concentrations camps of Hitler and Himmler have been a most important factor in the Church Unity Movement because of the sacrifices made in common.

We should take note here, moreover, of the fact that both Churches are striving to realize more fully in themselves the essential principles of Christianity. Consequently, Christians today, unlike their predecessors, are aware of the wholly unchristian character of the division between them; in particular we are aware of the grave precept found in the high-priestly prayer of our Lord *"ut omnes unum sint: that they all may be one"* (John 17:21). I must emphasize then the fact that this is an obligation imposed upon us. If we pay close attention to the meaning of the words, we will see that our Lord is saying simply that the world as a whole can come to have real faith in Him only when all Christians are perfectly united. The world will not be able to have real faith in our Lord until the followers of Christ are essentially united as the Father and the Son are. This is a fact of tremendous importance; serious indeed is the charge against us that for four hundred years we have taken a rather nonchalant attitude toward the schism in Christianity, a schism so scandalous, that it exposes us to the mockery of many. According to these words of our Lord, it was inevitable that faith should decline throughout the world as soon as the scandal of schism at the heart of Christianity became apparent to one and all. These words of our Lord lead us to conclude that the re-Christianization of the world is intimately bound up with the healing of the division between the Churches.

"That they all may be one!" Our Lord is not referring to some kind of horizontal leveling but to the need all have to be profoundly united to Him. The increasing sense of dogma manifest among contemporary Protestants is leading them to an awareness of the meaninglessness, theologically speaking, of talking of "churches" in the plural, in the sense that the preaching of one faith is no more justified than the preaching of any other.

In addition the increasingly frequent discussions between the churches that have taken place during the past twenty years have produced concrete results, as have the achievements of historical scholarship as well. Beyond a possession of similar views in purely historical matters, it is a heartening experience to see that comprehensive discussions concerning a new presentation of the Reformation, such as I engaged in, could be possible, without falling willy nilly into one or more basically insincere positions.

The question can be and has been asked, whether reflection on the events of history can radically influence life in our own day. In other words, can reflection on the historical data of the Reformation further the cause of union which occupies our interest today? The question is not correctly phrased because it seems to be oriented toward a program of action and this must be avoided at all costs. I have already mentioned that the distinctive note of optimism implicit in the present situation is due partly to the fact that we know how little we accomplish by mere busy hustling. Our task is at one and the same time simpler, yet much more profound. With truth, love, and sincere intellectual endeavor we must lay the foundations for a true and fair re-evaluation of the Reformation.

We must admit that the Protestant Churches of today are independent both of the Reformation and of questions of the justice or injustice of that movement. The events of the Reformation are facts of history with their own significance; as for the churches, they have had four hundred years in which to develop, change, and become involved in various ways with the culture of their age. The truths which the reformers regarded as essential are not only independent of subsequent developments but have, in fact, become dead letters. The Reformation itself was responsible for the fact that the explanation of the religious revolt is basically independent of the explanation of subsequent developments of that revolt. One of the most pernicious features of Protestantism is evident here: the individual Christian, subject to no authority but that of his own conscience, has to grapple with the words of Scripture on his own; for, even where the authority of the Church is recognized to the extent admitted by Luther, the basic Protestant attitude leads of necessity to an ultimate rejection of that authority.

In spite of this, however, the concrete situation of the Protestants churches and denominations does really depend on the question of whether the doctrines of the Reformers of the sixteenth century in opposition to those of the Roman Catholic Church were right or wrong. If the present day doctrines of the Protestant Churches are to be justified, they must be founded on the very arguments proposed by

the first Reformers. The earliest statements of the reformed
faith are still valid and wield a mighty influence in our
own day. Luther's personality and the new roads he opened
up are still the dominant influence in the Lutheran Church,
at least as the ideal it strives to regain.

In view of this fact, the following conclusion seems unavoidable: If, through a more profound study of pre-Reformation times, as well as of Luther's course of development, we can demonstrate that the Reformers broke with
the Church essentially because of misunderstandings and
an objectively incorrect grasp of the situation, the sincere
Protestant will be shaken to the depths of his religious consciousness. (By the word *Protestant* here, I wish to desig-
nate those who hold to the doctrines of the first Reformers
and not those who hold a fully autonomous, merely hu-
manitarian, ethical system.) The Protestant in this situation sees himself face to face with the fundamental problem
of human existence. To doubt this would be to affirm the
utter bankruptcy of the human spirit.

I.

The Causes of the Reformation

The Introduction sufficiently outlines our attitudes as we approach this study of the Reformation. We begin this study with a pertinent observation. If we are to discuss the causes of the Reformation with any objectivity, we must be ready to discuss a number of unpleasant aspects in the history of the Church. We will face these facts honestly and sincerely in the conviction that by so doing we best serve truth and hence our common Christianity. If, in the process, we are forced to direct adverse or severe criticism against the Church, or rather, against her leaders and members of a former age, we would ask the reader to note the spirit in which this criticism is made. At times, Catholics have taken a certain malicious pleasure in criticism; this, however, is not our own attitude. We will be critical but our desire is to help the Church as our Mother, the source of our life, prayer, and sacrifice.

If historical considerations are to penetrate to the heart of the issues, they cannot be restricted to the question of what happened, how individual events came to pass. They must penetrate and describe the genesis of these events. Historical study is fruitful only if the light of the intellect is focused on the whole past. This approach will be facilitated by examining the events to be treated from as broad a point of view as possible. Historical causality is not immediate causality.[1]

Martin Luther was the immediate cause of the Reformation, but behind this limited immediate cause stand a significant number of preparatory factors and conditions that alone can make possible the type of event that leaves its imprint on an age. This is true both for revolutionary movements and for the creative geniuses who mastermind them. It is certainly applicable to Martin Luther. The lively manifestation of the reforming spirit that made a reformer out of a Catholic monk apparently owes little to the individual theological elements assimilated by Luther in his studies. The phenomenon of the change in Luther's thinking was certainly not externally manifest, and his definitive break with the past proceeded immediately from irrational elements in his character. There is question here of a profound movement of a human spirit in its relations with God; this movement is neither explicable in terms of, nor necessarily connected with, individual historical details of theological thought. The event is mysterious. It be-

---

[1] The problems involved in historical causality are far more complicated than can be indicated here. To avoid possible misunderstandings, however, the following should be noted: Nothing except pure quantity, as a principle of enumeration, is univocal; reality has many facets. It is thus of the nature of historical causality to be multivalent. We will see, for example, that a personal spirituality of the late medieval period arose in a series of causes responsible for the reform movement; these took place within the Church as well as in the Reformation. It is frequently, if not always, difficult to see the extent of influence in any given event, especially what strata of society or periods of time are exempt from this influence. In other words, it is impossible to grasp the entire gamut of influence for any historical fact. In the following pages, therefore, when we speak of historical causality we limit our consideration to but one single series of effects. By the enumeration of these series of causes we by no means intend to provide a complete analysis of the period involved—that would be possible only by presenting a number of highly involved causal series.

gins in mystery and is shrouded in mystery up to the moment it appears. Yet we can show that Luther's definitive rupture with Rome was definitely connected with elements in the theology of the time; so close, in fact, is this bond that the rupture could never have occurred outside of that particular constellation of elements. If Luther had not been a monk, if his interests had not been theological, if his theological orientation had been that of St. Thomas or of the Roman Missal, rather than that of William of Ockham, his own inclination to reform would never have had the effect it did; the friction that provided the spark and led to the crisis that split Christendom would be utterly inexplicable. Luther's own anxiety over sin and judgment would never have reached critical proportions where they served to trigger and confirm his novel ideas, but even if they had, they would never have emerged from the confused world of inner conflict and become systematized and raised to the level of a history-molding force.

Now if we take the concept of historical cause in the wide sense indicated above, including both remote and proximate causality, then in the analysis of historical causes, the infinitely variegated pattern of history, the apparently arbitrary ebb and flow of historical development, we are led to a recognition of a new level which we might term historical necessity.

Note well that I say historical necessity, a type which I want to distinguish from absolute necessity in a most clear manner, for this belongs to a purely materialistic concept of history. Historical existence is never autonomous in the full sense of the word. Not even the most clear-cut forms or structures of secular life have full title to a place in the sun by reason of their purely historical existence. In other words "concrete" historical situations are not the only

things that contain elements of truth and justice, but so also
do error and injustice. This means that the coincidence of
a vast number of historical causes merely indicates that the
actualization of a specific event was necessary and unavoidable, but this is far from an exhaustive explanation of the
event.

In reference to the Reformation, when we fully list all
of its causes and show that a violent uprising against the
former Church was absolutely inevitable, we have still said
nothing about whether or not the new doctrines of the Reformers were justified or not.

The point that we wish to discuss is: How did the Reformation become possible? And by asking "how" we are
implicitly asking "why." More specifically we are asking:
In the family of Western nations, fully and consciously
committed to the Roman Church as their divinely appointed guide, how did factors, predominantly intellectual
and cultural, such as a new way of thinking, develop that
made it possible for the greater part of this community to
separate itself from the Church? What happened that made
it possible for entire peoples who knew only the Christianity of the Roman Church under papal authority conceive
of a form of Christianity outside of this Church without a
pope?

Note well that every description of a historical reality
has a tendency to be cast into a schematic form. The fullness of life cannot be encompassed by mere words, especially in the case of past events, where, at best, our information is meager. Discussions are limited by time and must
of necessity be restricted to sketching the broad outlines of
a picture. Throughout the discussions which follow, some,
well-acquainted with the history of the Reformation, will
look in vain for a fuller explanation of many points and

for definite reservations concerning others. In spite of this I shall carefully attempt to avoid any false statements or the impression that the whole gamut of problems is exhausted in this brief treatment.

A preliminary answer to our questions would be that the Reformation came to pass because of the disappearance of certain fundamental attitudes proper to the Middle Ages. This seems to be a rather obvious platitude, but, if correctly analyzed, this statement brings to our attention each of the vast number of elements that can be considered causes of the Reformation.

The concept, *medieval*, as it is usually used, was verified fully only for a period of brief duration. As soon as the Middle Ages, in the strict sense of the term, i.e., the High Middle Ages, emerged from the long fermenting process, which took place between the fifth and the tenth century and gradually came to full blossoming in the eleventh, a continual shifting of ideas on many subjects began in the minds of the people of the times. Viewed from the aspect of the history of the Church, this phenomenon appeared as the growth of a somewhat objective, disinterested attitude toward the Church, if not a movement of withdrawal in its regard. To analyze this attitude and movement is to present the causes of the Reformation in outline forms.

This movement progressed in many different aspects and appeared in the actions of loyal disciples of the Church as well as its resolute opponents. By far the most important fact to note is that a new disposition of dynamic factors took place within the Church.

With particular reference to the Reformation, a more objective view of the Church can be summed up as follows: Long before the Reformation elements of reform existed in the Roman Church and Western Christianity. To avoid misunderstandings, we use the term *reform* or *reformative* as a description of remote contributing forces. This has nothing to do with the much-abused term, "forerunners of the Reformation," applied, for example, to St. Francis or Savonarola, as types of evangelical piety.

Rather we mean this: Long before the Reformation within Western Christianity events occurred, measures were taken, and ideas proposed that facilitated, made possible, or even demanded the development of a sweeping revolt against the Church of Rome.

These ideas gradually permeated large areas of Christianity; consequently, men began to see that existence without papal authority was neither impossible nor unchristian. Thus when new doctrines were proposed in the sixteenth century, they no longer appeared utterly foreign to the climate of the times but were welcomed with enthusiasm. In other words when the Reformers of the sixteenth century proposed their doctrines and made their demands, many elements they proposed found a sympathetic response in attitudes that were already part and parcel of the makeup of Western Europe.

To express the same idea differently, many events in the centuries before the Reformation contributed in an important way to the actual realization of that event by Luther and the other reformers. Without the preparation afforded during these centuries by means of these "pre-reformation" elements, the Reformation would never have occurred. And without taking into account the all-pervasive character of these pre-Reformation elements, it is impossible to understand the facts of the Reformation itself.

We can illustrate these pre-Reformation elements in many ways because they appeared in many forms. We will select three of the more important ones and apply our thesis to them.

The first indication of the course that history was to take concerns the unity of the medieval world. The Reformation signalled the breakdown of Christian unity in the West; however, long before this, unity had been weakened in its very foundations and the way had been prepared for collapse at the time of the Reformation.

The unity of the Middle Ages has often been exaggerated. The medieval period, in the strict sense of the word, lasted from perhaps one hundred and fifty to two hundred years. Not only was the period of development up to the eleventh century an extremely slow and at times sporadic growth, but in the thirteenth century itself so many dispersive factors appeared on the medieval scene that from that time onwards medieval unity in the full sense of the word was already a thing of the past. Yet the unity of the Christian Church in the West was a reality throughout the entire period known as the Middle Ages, a powerful unitive factor, and, despite what we have said, stronger than either before or after; for, in the last analysis, it was based on a unity of one faith under one ecclesiastical regime. Another facet of this unity, a subordination to one ecclesiastical regime, appeared in the unity of Church and State, *sacerdotium et imperium.*

This latter form of medieval unity bears further examination. Although a source of many a conflict, this unity was by no means an arbitrary or chance state of affairs. It was an expression of the essence of medieval society, a logical development of the union of the Church with the Germanic peoples. The weakening of this form of medieval unity was, of necessity, a weakening of the force which impressed this unity—the Christian Church.

This process, tragically enough, was furthered to a significant degree by the Papacy itself. One aspect of the process is manifest in the fact that it was the popes of the period

who caused the downfall of that specifically medieval phenomenon, the Holy Roman Empire. Although its downfall
may be lamented, it is hard to say that the Papacy was not
justified in locking horns with the German emperors of
the day. What the Papacy objected to was a novel, secular-
ized concept of the Empire which left no room for an independent Church or an independent Papacy. The popes of
that day fought for the independence of the Church; their
cause was just and so was their victory.

Unfortunately it was a Pyrrhic victory. Viewed from the
standpoint of the Church itself, it left a vacuum and represented the downfall of a powerful secular arm of ecclesiastical authority that led to a dangerous imbalance of power.
From the political standpoint, it represented the end of
universal political authority. Consequently a spirit of petty
and egoistic nationalism was free to turn against the
Church, and, in particular, against the papal possessions
in Italy. On the other hand, the popes of the day chose
precisely this moment to press to the limit their claims in
the political and economic sphere. They were encouraged
no doubt by the fact that their long-time opponents, the
German emperors, no longer stood in their way. In so
doing, they laid themselves open to attack by various national powers that entered the historical scene at the time.
These attacks were not only successful but, viewed from a
purely temporal standpoint, justifiable.

The implications of the papal victory over the German
emperors soon became clear, for during that struggle, the
Papacy relied to a great extent on the support of France.
This tendency, which had begun in the twelfth century, led
ultimately to the Avignon Papacy of the fourteenth century.
The significance of the so-called Avignon exile cannot be
grasped by regarding it merely as the transfer of the papal
residence from Rome to Avignon for several decades; it

signified rather the close dependence of the Papacy on France. The pope no longer had the freedom of movement and breadth of view proper to the Patriarch of the West; he had rather become a French Court bishop. It is quite easy to see that in Germany, for example, people would no longer be as willing to recognize the authority or heed the words of the pope; the inevitable reaction was a diminished loyalty to the Papacy. We must judge this phenomenon from the standpoint of the fourteenth century when the medieval world-view was still prevalent, and not from that of our own day. In the case of the vast majority of people, their attitude toward the popes remained unchanged. History, however, does teach us that values change quite subtly, while appearances and conscious attitudes require a longer period to catch up.

Another noteworthy feature about the Avignon exile was that the Avignon popes certainly had no intention of curbing their universal and far-reaching claims in the temporal sphere. In fact they pushed these claims to the limit precisely when the spirit of awakening nationalism made this policy extremely unwise. This was no longer the former medieval universalism in the religious sense. It was no accident but rather an historical necessity that Avignon saw the development by the Papacy of the complex financial system which seems to be nothing but the perversion and secularization of the medieval spirit of universalism.

Previously the pope had been enveloped in a religious aura which protected and raised him far above the level of all other princes; but now he could be discussed, treated, and attacked like any other prince. This wide-ranging movement away from the Papacy was most significant in that it strengthened the feeling among various peoples that their independence of the Papacy was quite justified.

We have to keep in mind the fact that medieval man

did not clearly distinguish between the spiritual and temporal, between eternal truth and its historically conditioned manifestations. We need think only of the long struggle over lay investiture that occurred before men were able to distinguish the sphere of competence of the Church from that of the state. Before this concept could be clarified, centuries of controversy were needed. Even in the thirteenth and fourteenth centuries, the Roman Curia made the unfortunate mistake of confusing absolute papal primacy of jurisdiction in dogmatic matters with papal temporal power as it was historically verified and justified in the medieval period. In fact, the Curia took pains to link its temporal power as closely as possible to primacy in matters of dogma so that proofs that justified the latter were called into service to bolster the former. All available means were used to clothe temporal power with the aura of the divine, and thus to give it some justification.

This unfortunate confusion had an inevitable result. As the operative forces of history led new and politically independent nations to rise justifiably against papal temporal power and crowned their struggle with success, unavoidably, yet unfortunately, the movement turned against the supremacy of the pope in purely dogmatic matters. Not that it was justified in doing so. The point is that it did, and to a great extent those tendencies of the Papal Curia mentioned above were responsible, because they had fostered the confusion of two distinct areas of authority.

The Papacy lost its privileged position and the unity of the medieval period was weakened. The course of events accustomed people to periodic bitter struggles with the Papacy. To be sure it was thoroughly in accord with the medieval spirit for the Christian to be quite free in criticizing his Church without dreaming of harming the unity of that Church, or denying his subjection to the pope. However, the distinction in matters of this kind is rather delicate; the day easily arrives when it will no longer be made. Because of the developments previously mentioned, that day eventually came. Radical criticism became possible and whole nations withdrew from their loyalty to the Papacy. A careful study of the documents involved shows how the battle waged by the various national states against papal claims in the temporal sphere moved imperceptibly but continuously in the direction of disagreement in the sphere of dogmatic truths.

The significance of the break-up of medieval unity in the thirteenth century, but even more during the Avignon period, is evident in the most distinctive historical consequence of the Avignon Papacy: the Great Western Schism. The real meaning of this event may not be immediately apparent. It can be somewhat superficially described as a period when there were two popes, each with his own Curia, one residing in Rome, the other in Avignon. This situation in which both contenders claimed to be pope (at one time the number increased so that many spoke of the "cursed trinity") was in the main corrected by the efforts of the German Emperor Sigismund at the Council of Constance in 1414. These statements are true, but the account they give is sketchy and superficial; they tell us nothing of the real significance of the Schism.

The real significance of the Western Schism rests in the fact that for decades there was an almost universal uncertainty about where the true pope and the true Church were to be found. For several decades, both popes had excommunicated each other and his followers; thus all Christendom found itself under sentence of excommunication by at least one of the contenders. Both popes referred to their rival claimant as the Antichrist, and to the Masses celebrated by them as idolatry. It seemed impossible to do anything about this scandalous situation, despite sharp protests from all sides, and despite the radical impossibility of having two valid popes at the same time. Time and time again, the petty selfishness of the contenders blocked any solution.

The split caused by the Western Schism was far from being merely the concern of theologians; no area of public or private life remained untouched; even the economic sphere was affected, mainly because of disputes in regard to the possession of benefices. Provinces of the Church, religious orders, universities, even individual monasteries and parish houses were divided. For decades, all experienced this profound division in all sectors of daily life. Good people on both sides, even saints, were not only unable to bring about unity, but in their allegiance to one or the other of the contenders they themselves were in sharp opposition. We find, for example, St. Catherine of Siena on the Roman side and St. Vincent Ferrer on that of Avignon. Furthermore, the settlement of the Schism at the Council of Constance did not really solve the problem. The triumph of the Conciliar Theory at Constance, and even more at Basel, extended the life span of the Schism from 1378 to 1448, when it finally came to an end in the person of the Antipope Felix V. The confusion and uncertainty about the valid pope and the true Church is manifest in the amazing twists in the allegiance of Nicolaus of Cusa and Aeneas Silvio dei Piccolomini, later to become Pius II, both of whom had begun by defending the Conciliar Theory in its most radical form.

This was an experience shared by the entire West—one which would leave its imprint in Western consciousness for a long time to come. The memory of this experience was still fresh a century later. It is not too difficult to see the effects of the Western Schism in preparing the way for the doctrines of the Reformation. When Luther asserted that the pope of Rome was not the true successor of Saint Peter and that the Church could do without the Papacy, in his mind and in their essence these were new doctrines, but the distinctive element in them was not new and thus they struck a sympathetic resonance in the minds of many. Long before the Reformation itself, the unity of the Christian Church in the West had been severely undermined.

Another illustration of the imminence of the break-up appears in the fact that the Reformation was the expression of far-reaching discontent among many elements in the Church; here again we have proof of the existence of "reformative" elements in the Church long before Luther's time.

As early as 1200 the appeal for reform in head and members was being insistently pressed in the Church, together with the call for a return to the simplicity of apostolic times. This movement was not confined to certain sectors of society; not just a few groups of independent Christians were making their discontent known. Rather, it is of special importance to realize that these demands for reform, these indications of criticism came from within the Church, from the most loyal servants of the Papacy—even from those who were dedicated to an exaggerated ideal of papal power. These demands were frequently put forward in a most radical form which we find somewhat surprising and which bear further examination.

We usually look upon the reign of Innocent III as representing the high-water mark of ecclesiastical power during the medieval period—the time when all Western Christendom was more closely united than ever under the

supreme temporal and spiritual sovereignty of the pope.
The Lateran Council of 1215 admirably expressed the
splendor and the universal character of the Papacy, but we
must not forget that there was another side to the picture:
the pope himself declared that the main task of the Council
was to bring about reform.

Whenever there is mention of reform in the Church,
Catholics have a tendency to think of trivial changes, at
most touching upon some minor points in the aesthetic
sphere. We ordinarily feel that evil cannot be deeply rooted
in the Church, for after all our Lord assured her of the
guidance of the Holy Spirit, and her holiness is just as
surely guaranteed as her truth. This last statement is true
and on this guarantee of the stability of the truth and holiness of the Church rests her superiority in doctrine to all
those churches that have yielded in some degree to subjectivism. But it is equally true that the Church's holiness
and possession of the truth is definitely restricted to the
sacraments and to dogma in the strict sense of the word.
With these exceptions, absolutely everything in the Church
is subject to weakness, misuse, and error. So true is this,
that time and time again throughout the centuries the very
existence of the Church has been threatened. Today Catholics are often in such an unfavorable position that they
are somewhat hesitant to admit these deep-seated weaknesses in their Church. The greatest figures in the history
of the Church, including the greatest popes, felt no such
restraint: they often spoke of the imminent decline of the
Church. From this it appears that the possibility and necessity of reform in the Church corresponds perfectly to the
earnest and universal appeal of the New Testament for
metanoia—repentance.

This profound relationship was understood at the be-

ginning of the thirteenth century as is clear from the life of
St. Francis of Assisi, the great contemporary, if not opponent, of Pope Innocent III. In the vision at San Damiano
he had heard the words, "My house is falling to pieces;
build it up again!" Taking these words quite literally,
Francis began by rebuilding the little chapel but the story
of his whole life and work is eloquent testimony to the fact
that he also understood it as a divine command to bring
about a far-reaching moral and religious renewal in the
Church.

For his part, Francis of Assisi did accomplish a reform
within the Church and the effect of his creative personality
was felt for centuries. Yet he was but one of a number of
reform-minded Saints of his own time. The fourteenth century is quite notable, too, for worthwhile achievements in
the field of Christian perfection. One need but mention
various preachers of penance, founders of orders, and reformers of religious life to realize that the fifteenth century
also was concerned with accomplishing "a reform in head
and members." Despite all of this, despite genuine holiness,
despite various attempts and minor successes in the direction of reform, during the thirteenth, fourteenth, and fifteenth centuries as a whole, things did not get better but
worse.

This state of affairs did not have any single cause. The
process of deterioration proceeded with almost measured
steps and, given the situation of the time, it could hardly
have been avoided unless those who led the Church had all
been saints. The reason is that implicit in the medieval
world view lay a tremendous temptation: medieval man
made no adequate distinction between the Church and the
world, the man consecrated to God and the military man,
the spiritual and the temporal. In all of these spheres, the

temptations to power and pleasure were almost irresistible
as events show only too clearly.

In speaking of Avignon, we mentioned its policies in
regard to ecclesiastical benefices; because of these policies,
the Papal Curia of the day became one of the most heavily
capitalized ventures of its day and certainly the most significant.

It was inevitable that in this close union of divine grace
with the mammon of iniquity, divine grace was bound to
suffer and the door would be opened for simoniacal abuses.
As proof of this we have the extremely bitter criticism directed at the Curia, not only by saints, such as Catherine
of Siena and Brigit of Sweden, but by members of the
Curia such as Alvarez Pelayo who warned bitterly, "Those
who rule the Church are wolves; they are glutted with
blood, and the soul of every one of them is stained with
blood." In Avignon that system began which later reached
its high point with the culture-minded popes of the Renaissance; a system in which the values of money, power, and
pleasure had to a large measure supplanted those of prayer,
pastoral activity, and the priestly life. We will see that
almost all of the abuses of the Late Middle Ages can be
traced back to Avignon.

We find one extremely significant indication of how
early a deep dissatisfaction with conditions in the Church,
with clericalism and curialism, appeared; of how strongly
the democratic spirit of the laity manifested itself in demanding radical changes. This indication lies in the fact
that in the year 1325, one hundred and fifty years before
the birth of Luther, almost two hundred years before the
Reformation became an accomplished fact, a book such as
Defensor Pacis could appear. The doctrine of this book was
in radical opposition to that of the Church. To be sure, the

book appeared before its time; so much so that it did not
have any great effect. The significant point is that the book
would not have been possible if it did not represent an important theological current that remained underground. Its
thought was Averroistic in tone, and tragically enough, the
book attacked the Church on the grounds of the same
Aristotelian concept of natural law which the Papal Curia
had used as a foundation for its theory of papal temporal
power. The only difference was that here the concept of
natural law was once more isolated and treated autono-
mously as it had been in pagan philosophy.

In the year in which this book appeared, Wycliffe had
been born—Wycliffe, so radically independent of Rome
and so insistent in calling the pope the Antichrist.

Complaints against the Curia, already being heard at
the beginning of the fourteenth century, mounted as time
went on. By the end of the fifteenth century, Europe was a
hotbed of discontent over the dominance of Rome and the
clergy. Sometimes the cry was raised impatiently and an-
grily, at other times sadly, and often quite boldly, but the
cry was raised against churchmen, oppression, greed, arbitrariness and, above all, against single-minded dedication to
pleasure.

Naturally it must be asked whether all these complaints
were justified or whether a spirit of unrestrained and egotis-
tical criticism had exaggerated the faults of the clergy
beyond all bounds. Nevertheless, no matter to what extent
this criticism may have been without justification, much
remained that was scandalous and unchristian. From the
historical point of view, the important fact is that, justified
or not, the hue and cry against Rome had been raised. The
spirit of discontent was rife; it made itself felt in literature,
the pulpit, pamphlets, songs, and parliaments. In their de-

mands and invective many went beyond all bounds; even
the most radical criticism of the Church was assured of
universal applause. From this it is clear that large numbers
were ready to rise against Rome and against the privileges
of the clergy. When Luther appeared, he seemed to offer a
definitive solution to the long overdue problem of reform
which, as all agreed, was absolutely necessary.

Finally, we come to the most important point of all.
The Reformation certainly represented a denial of the doctrines of the Catholic faith; yet as paradoxical as it might
seem, here too the foundation had been laid for some time.
It might seem that this could not happen within the Catholic Church, that doctrines of this type would, by that very
fact, no longer be Catholic. Such a view is an oversimplification.

Whenever a point is of critical importance, I am always
in favor of presenting it in such a form that it seems almost
impossible to prove. Then we have something to work with,
and this is what I wish to do here. We are not interested
in the truly heretical movements of the Middle Ages or in
those which had a definitely heretical coloring, such as
Arabic pantheism, the Waldensians, Cathari, Wycliffe and
Hus. We are interested in movements inside the Church—
movements which can, without restriction, be attributed to
the Church of Rome. With these limitations understood, I
would propose the following thesis: Within the Roman
Catholic Church, from the fourteenth century on, an ever-
increasing theological uncertainty had made itself felt, so
that by the end of the Middle Ages the whole situation
was characterized by a great deal of confusion in theological matters.

Now to study this thesis in detail would demand a number of precisions that could only be treated in a history of

the theology of the late medieval period; there is no such
definitive history at this time. All I would wish to indicate
is that the thesis, as I propose it, applies with truth in vary-
ing degrees throughout the nations of Western Europe. In
the case of Italy and Spain where the Augustinian and
Thomistic traditions were still strong, the thesis was verified
to an insignificant degree, compared with the nations of
Central Europe and England.

People have been slow to recognize the importance of
this theological confusion; yet, in the truest sense of the
word, it is the one cause that made the Reformation possible. Here, as in many other cases, we must make an effort
to understand that the foundation on which the Reformation was built, and the whole progress of the movement
itself, was dependent not only on elements in the religious
life of the time but, to an even more important degree, on
strictly theological considerations.

Some may object that the Creeds, the Confessions of
Faith used by all were still Catholic, and that thereby
uniformity of belief was still guaranteed; but this would be
too superficial a view for our present discussions. Even
today Catholics and Lutherans use the same formulas in
confessing the divinity of our Lord. For this reason Johann
Sebastian Bach had no difficulty in using the text of the
Roman Missal in writing his Mass, without sacrificing the
integrity of his Protestant faith. It is in the content of each
article of the Creed that we must search for those points
which distinguish the Catholic from the Protestant.

Implicit, too, in our thesis is the contention that the
numerous theological systems that flourished toward the
end of the medieval period were a sign not only of the
breadth and richness of the tradition, but even more a sign
of the intrinsic contradictions possible within the frame-

work of the Church itself. Too much was demanded of the Catholic ideal of universality, with the result that universality itself was in danger of ceasing to be Catholic.

In proof of our thesis, we will begin by noting the increasingly arbitrary character of the theological constructions and disputations of the period which were often enough pushed far beyond reasonable limits. This process went hand in hand with certain regrettable factors in the treatment of other disciplines subsidiary to theology.

This development is the expression of a process of isolation that infected the theology of the day; it may properly be called the withdrawal of theology from the sacramental life of the Church. This point deserves emphasis, for the search for truth in theology is profoundly different from the search for truth in other fields. The scholar working by himself is simply incapable of attaining theological truth, for this truth belongs essentially to the sphere of faith. It is nourished by the life of faith—it is an expression of the life of the Church. Whenever theology loses or weakens its vital link with the Church and its sacramental life, the search for theological truth inevitably suffers. The sacramental life of the Church had lost much of its vigor; people in the late medieval period approached the sacraments all too infrequently; the Mass and the Holy Eucharist came to be understood in a superficial or moralistic sense. Consequently, theological scholarship was threatened as it thereby became impossible for theology to attain its goal.

This is easier to grasp if we recall the apparently obvious but often forgotten fact that truth is threatened not only by crass error, but also by the weakness and apathy of those who defend it.

Two extremely instructive examples of this autonomous type of theological scholarship which was separated from the sacramental life of the Church in the late medieval period are quite pertinent to the theme of this entire book. The first was Desiderius Erasmus. Although a priest and a theologian, he took little account of the sacramental life of the Church, either in theory or practice. His basic attitude in exegesis was that human scholarship was the most important requisite for the interpretation of Scripture. The second was Martin Luther who laid such emphasis on his doctoral degree in claiming both the right and duty to propose and defend his theological insights.

The theological theories that developed in this period are best represented by the work of the English Franciscan William of Ockham and his followers. Research in this area, by the way, has only begun to scratch the surface. Under the same general heading, I would also include the further developments of Ockhamism in the fifteenth century, for, although defended by loyal sons of the Church, it, too, was destructive of true theology. Implicit in its content and methods were principles which, if pushed to their logical conclusions, would inevitably lead to a denial of the Church's doctrines. It is my assertion that Ockhamism, as understood here, was no longer fully Catholic.

It is extremely difficult to define what we mean by fully Catholic. On the one hand we have the old formula of Vincent of Lerin: "That is fully Catholic which has been believed always, everywhere and by all." But on the other hand we know that in the course of the centuries new doctrines have been formulated. Nevertheless, it is not my intention, as certain Protestant critics have suggested, to use the Tridentine definitions as norms by which to measure the theology of the late medieval period and of Martin Luther.

Instead, I would invoke a certain basic core of dogma which was regarded as incontestably Catholic in the full sense of the word. The basic viewpoint of Augustine or Thomas Aquinas would certainly belong to this dogmatic core. It will be even more useful for our purposes if we limit ourselves to a source which both in itself and in its external expression was the same in the fifteenth century as it is today: the Roman Missal, which Luther used in the same form as we do today. Measured by this norm, Ockhamism is no longer a fully Catholic theology.

The Missal knows nothing of an arbitrary God; it knows nothing of a God who is merely a severe and threatening judge; it knows nothing of a God who acts only from a sense of punitive justice; it knows nothing of man capable of offering satisfaction to God by relying merely on his own human powers. On the contrary, the Missal shows us a man who is at one and the same time a child of God and a sinner, who does not rely on his own merits, but in loving reverence seeks God the Father through the Son and His grace and by so doing is elevated by God to the supernatural life.

Ockhamism, on the other hand, teaches the existence of an arbitrary God, instead of a God who is our Father; it teaches of a God who without objective grounds predetermines some men to heaven and others to hell; of a God who in the most arbitrary fashion determined which acts were to be good and which were to be evil and who was perfectly capable of having reversed the order.

Ockhamism, as held by Pierre d'Ailly, Gabriel Biel, and Gregory of Rimini, is committed to an extreme exaggeration of man's part in the process of justification and of his relation to an arbitrary God. The inevitable theological conclusion is a cheapening of divine grace; this, of course, would give a false orientation to Christianity as a whole.

Finally, Ockhamism, which denied the authority of Aristotle, was characterized by an exaggerated separation of nature and supernature, to the point of holding the principle of a two-fold truth—something can be theologically true because it is contained in revelation, and philosophically false because it could be refuted or proved impossible by reason.

It is true that Ockhamism was condemned at Avignon in the fourteenth century, but the little that we know of that condemnation does not give the impression that the real danger of Ockhamism was recognized at all. Actually, the condemnation did not seem to be against Ockham the theologian, but against Ockham's theory of the relation of Church and State because this theory was attractive to the Emperor Ludwig the Bavarian. At any rate, theologians of the period were not usually aware of the impending danger. Rather, a nominalism that lay behind Ockham's theology became a powerful factor within scholastic theology, and where it prevailed, scholastic theology perished. Nominalism was not applied rigorously to the area of supernatural truth. Its individualizing, atomizing tendencies, which resolved various dialectic unities and then exaggerated their separate elements, are unsuited to dealing with a sacramental organism like the Church or to reaching any intelligibility on the theological level. For the nominalist, the Church is nothing more than the sum of all the faithful; they constitute the Church. They do not owe their faith to a Church conceived as something more than the mass of the faithful. As Clémanges said, in their view it was possible that the faith could decline to the point where only one old woman would be left to profess it. The theological implications of such a theory in promoting radical democ-

racy in the Church and in eliminating the mediating function of the priesthood (rightly understood) are, if followed
to their logical conclusions, inevitable.

In many ways, these consequences are manifest in
Luther. As a point of departure, they brought about an explosive spiritual crisis in Luther's early life and strongly
affected Luther's whole outlook. This is evidenced by his
war on human reason, his theory of imputation, or again
by his battles against the theologians of the Catholic
Church on the question of the Holy Eucharist and the Sacrifice of the Mass.

This was precisely the tragedy of Luther's disputations
with Eck; both of them thought in nominalistic categories.
Luther was quite logical in proceeding from these concepts to a denial of Catholic doctrine; using these same
concepts, Eck was not able to justify theologically the theses
that he maintained. He heaped argument on argument in his
attempts to prove the Catholic doctrine concerning the
Sacrifice of the Mass and his whole argument proved
nothing. In retrospect we might ask whether it was not
precisely this theologically unsatisfactory character of Eck's
argument that strengthened Luther's conviction that he
himself possessed the fullness of revelation to a greater
degree than his opponent who represented the Church of
Rome.

The theological confusion of the late medieval period
is particularly evident in the increasing obscurity of the
idea of papal primacy. Before considering this problem,
we must return to our former discussion of the Great
Western Schism and of the Conciliar Theory which had such
far-reaching effects on the theological thought of the period.

In general, the loss of papal prestige and the low esteem
in which papal decisions were held were necessary condi-

tions for the acceptance of the doctrines of the Reformation. The gradual lessening of papal prestige could serve as a heading under which all the causes of the Reformation might be grouped. We could follow every detail of the process, observing how the aura of respect which had enveloped the Roman Pontiff had been abused, with the cooperation of the Roman Curia; how the pope had simply become another prince, who was attacked with the same weapons and as justifiably as any other prince. We might note the explosive issues implicit in the maintenance and exaggeration of papal claims beyond the time when they had strict historical justification. We would then see that the understandable reaction to these papal policies soon assumed revolutionary proportions in the case of Boniface VIII and his struggle against Philip the Fair of France. We would have to go into the loss of power and prestige which was the immediate consequence of the secular universalism of the popes as manifested in their political and economic battles with various nations. We would then see that there was a notable link between the secularization of papal jurisdictional primacy and its loss of authority in the strictly theological sphere.

It is true that nationalistic and sectional pride in every part of the Church after the fourteenth century played a significant rôle in the disregard of papal authority, but the Curia itself must bear some of the responsibility for the confusion and the obscurity. All sorts of arbitrary actions on the part of the Curia shook the confidence of the faithful; all sorts of abuses could be found in its worldly life. Above all, papal power, particularly in the secular sphere, was stressed beyond all limit. This exaggeration of papal power on the part of the Curia had as its inevitable reaction a minimizing of papal power by all others concerned. Most

importantly, the exaggerations of papal power in every
matter tended to blur the lines that separated the specifically medieval phenomenon of the universal power of the
Papacy and papal primacy in matters of dogma and ecclesiastical jurisdiction. The Curia itself mingled both elements
in its decisions and often thoroughly confused them. The
result was a mistaken notion of the essential content of the
idea of papal primacy that is noticeable on any number of
occasions at the end of the medieval period and at the beginning of the sixteenth century. This confusion ran the
gamut from extreme exaggeration of the essential meaning
of primacy to an utter denial of primacy in any sense of
the word. Both positions showed that far too much was
being included in the notion, that its true content was being
neglected, with the inevitable result that dogmatic primacy
suffered.

In discussing difficult problems of this type one might
be tempted to oversimplify by asserting that in the final
analysis papal primacy ceased to be recognized by many
because of the opposition of open or secret enemies of the
Church. But the fact of the matter is that all of these events
took place within the framework of the Church. Among
all the German princes of the early days of the Reformation, there was no more loyal son of the Church than the
Elector Count George of Saxony. On the occasion of the
disputation at Leipzig, in 1519, he had both Luther and
Eck to dinner, and, in accordance with the main object of
the disputation, the conversation turned to the question of
papal primacy. Today it is clear to us that everything depends on whether papal primacy is of divine or of human
institution, but it would seem that these distinctions seemed
quite incidental to the good Elector George. When the
argument between the two theologians seemed to be lasting

too long, he brought the dispute to an end with the naïve and untheological comment that, whether by divine or human institution, the pope was still the pope.

Finally we would have to include in our survey those elements of the new humanism which endanger dogma; more will be said on this topic later on.

The Council of Trent bears eloquent testimony to the confusion and uncertainty which became so widespread; hours of sometimes bitter dispute were needed to come to agreement on decisions in the most important matters which were to serve as a foundation for the necessary polemic as well as for the ordinary positive preaching of the Church.

In order to see the real significance of all these developments we would have to examine the practical attitude of the Curia of the Renaissance popes, especially in the battle waged by the Curia against the Reformation. Its outstanding characteristic was lack of interest in matters of dogma. Despite certain formalities of expression in Curial communications, it is a most consoling thought for Catholics to realize that the truth did not perish even though no one seemed very much interested in it.

Theological confusion soon emerged from the classroom and affected international politics, the relations of the Church with the various national powers, and the government of the Church itself. The dangers involved are quite evident if we follow the course of the struggle of the Papal Curia against the Reformation; in fact the damage that resulted from this struggle can be understood only in this light. Equally dangerous was the ecclesiastical policy of Emperor Charles V at the time of the imperial assembly at Augsburg in 1530. (The assembly itself was powerfully influenced by the ideas of Erasmus, through the Emperor

himself, his sisters, and Melancthon and Campeggio.) This
became clear in attempts at reconciliation during the 1540's
that were based on the principle of the least common dogmatic denominator.

There are innumerable examples of the extent to which
confusion reigned among the people and the lower clergy
on the very basic question of the Mass as well as practical
theological matters up to the high water mark of the Reformation and later. Without doubt the preaching, propaganda, and practice of the reformers were responsible for
much of this confusion, but the ground had already been
prepared.

In summary at the end of the medieval period the pre-
vailing confusion in theology became so acute that it was
quite easy for a theologically independent mind to be in
fact a heretical one.

This is not to say that it was impossible to find out
what the true doctrine was or to profess it in its fullness,
but there was a necessary condition. To employ the term
used from the time of Ignatius of Loyola, one had to think
with the Church. Unfortunately medieval theology did not
possess a treatise on the nature of the Church. Of course
there were circles in which men did think with the Church
in a way which is inspiring even today; if I had time I
would like to contrast a few with the main group of Catholic theologians who engaged in controversy during the Reformation. In this latter group, few progressed beyond the
mere possession of orthodox opinions to the point where
their lives and actions were dominated by a religious and
theological heritage. One that must be mentioned is the
learned Abbess Caritas Pirkheimer of Nürnberg. This
woman had a secure grasp of Catholic doctrine that was
both exact and rich. Her memoirs are worth reading.

We have now come to the point where it is necessary to begin filling in our general outline of the causes of the Reformation. We should now follow the course of this movement in the areas of politics, government of the Church, and the socio-economic sphere to become familiar with the gradual stabilizing of forces in the various areas. However, time is limited and we will confine our discussion to religious and intellectual life in the fifteenth century, turning first to the immediate causes of the Reformation at work in these areas. As the subject of our discussion becomes narrower, our treatment of the entire historical scene will be even more jejune than it has been up to now. We are interested in historical factors in the fifteenth century only insofar as they contributed to the Reformation, remembering all the while that the positive elements, though not wanting in Germany, had far greater historical importance in Spain and in Italy.

The fact that we emphasize factors in the intellectual and religious life of the times does not mean that political factors were unimportant and had no part in bringing about the Reformation. Not only were political events important in the external manifestation of the Reformation and in the spread of its doctrines and influence, but the development of what may be called the territorial Church in Germany in the fifteenth century was a decisive factor in the spread of the Reformation. Without the territorial Church as it developed in the fifteenth century, and as it played its political rôle in the sixteenth century during the Reformation, Luther might have appeared, but the Reformation would never have succeeded.

An examination of intellectual and religious life in the fifteenth century will show that herein lies the true explanation for the events of the time and their historical causes.

Once this is understood, it is possible to grasp the real significance of the causal chain that led to an extremely complex structure of men, attitudes, and events which we call the Reformation.

In the intellectual sphere, the fifteenth century was characterized in Germany as an age of contrasts, an age of collapse, and an age profoundly concerned with renewing its spirit. Of course history is full of overlapping periods; many elements of the historical scene are always fading into the past, while others remain vital elements in an historical process. However, some ages seem more complete in themselves, more static, while in others ties with the past have been weakened as men searched for new landmarks, new standards. The fifteenth century was such an age. Precisely as an age of contrasts, the fifteenth century was an impressive example of the extent to which medieval unity was a thing of the past and an indication of the dangers implicit in the uncertainty which pervaded the age itself. It is this latter element that explains why the old ways, the old ideas or ideals, yielded so completely to the new.

Traces of opposition abounded everywhere. Even today when we look at the architecture of the period with its profusion of involved and bewildering lines, sharply hewn clefts and weaving vaults, we have the impression of looking at the expression of a perplexed and troubled spirit.

The contradictions characteristic of the age appear in a most significant form in the fact that a true and rich concept of Catholic life, nourished by personal contact with the life and work of our Lord, flourished at the same time as a process of fragmentation as evidenced in the externalism of ordinary Catholic practice, in nominalism, humanism and in a segment of Thomism which had lost its vital contact with the past.

In the area of worship we find the same fragmentation expressed in a form which is especially noteworthy for us today, in the multiplication of the one high altar and the one Mass common to all (*vinculum unitatis!*), by the erection of side altars and the proliferation of private Masses. This spirit of individualism and fragmentation increased in the fifteenth century as the social organism split into a great number of guilds and crafts, each with its own altar, its own saint, its own feast day and its own Mass. All of this represented a dangerous division in the people of God; the picture is completed by the addition of many "family altars" that existed only for a given family and "their" Masses.

In the intellectual and spiritual life of the time, we can, for our purposes, summarize the opposing forces at work under three headings: scholasticism, humanism, and the influence of Nicolaus of Cusa. Scholasticism had split into every variety from Thomism to Ockhamism. Many forms of humanism were current, with all the good and bad features of a new and quite precocious movement. Cardinal Nicolaus of Cusa was at one and the same time a scholastic and a humanist, but too complex a figure to be included in either category. The intellectual currents of which he was a representative did not have a great influence on the Reformation. Thus his life and work are not pertinent to our discussion, but we should note that much could be learned from him that would be of use in the dialog between the churches. He is the master of the *complexio oppositorum,* an accomplished dialectical thinker, who can teach us much about the way in which the philosophical and theological foundations for union might be laid.

The fifteenth century was an age of profound disquiet —a disquiet implicit in all the opposing tensions which were at the same time its cause and expression. From this

point of view it is a classical example of a troubled age
that can no longer commit itself fully to former values and
ideals. It is important to note that the disquiet did not have
its origin in the serene confidence that a bright new world
was just around the corner; it sprang rather from a state
of anxiety. On the surface of things, humanism stood ready
to usher in a golden age, but pessimism and anxiety lay at
the heart of its world view. If we cast a critical eye on life
as a whole, it seemed that nothing was quite certain any
more. On the sheer physical level life and health were
threatened: syphilis and the plague swept through Europe
from 1486 to 1530; in one year thirty thousand people
died in the city of London. The same uncertainty affected
economic and political life; thus men were especially concerned about the future life. Men were wracked with anxiety over the possibility of eternal damnation, trembled in
expectation of the punishments that would be meted out
at the Last Judgment. This disquiet is apparent in the pas-
sionate and patient longing evidenced in the art of Riemenschneider, in the incessant economic complaints of the
lower classes throughout Germany, and in dangerous, revolutionary tendencies. The movement was essentially a religious and theological one that naturally found expression
in these fields. Any number of examples can be given. One
was the great popularity of pilgrimages, the urge to be on
the move as Thomas à Kempis expresses it. This spirit was
the sign of the instability of the spiritual life of the times
that could have most dangerous consequences, and it led
to many otherwise inexplicable outbreaks of a veritable
"salvation mania" on the part of large masses of the people.
We have another example in the great number of ecclesiastical foundations made at the time for the eternal salvation of the donors, and in the apocalyptic literature of the

day which mingled dire threats and radical programs to in-
sure salvation. This was the age when the great preachers
of penance made their most radical appeals for renuncia-
tion of the world. Even the art of the period has elements of
uncertainty and doubt, and the architecture, particularly
in the portals and baptistries, exhibits a mad confusion of
lines which escape harmonic resolution. In this connection,
the Lübeck painting of the Last Supper immediately comes
to mind; the painting succeeds in portraying the whole
range of problems of the pre-Reformation days by the attitude it expresses toward the reigning pope. Similar mention might be made of the altar at Isenheim where the crucified Lord is pictured as a victim of the plague.

Many have underestimated the disquiet of the age,
feeling that before the Reformation such an "un-Catholic"
movement would have been impossible. Such an attitude of
well-meant naïveté simply makes it impossible to understand the real nature of the sickness that may afflict any
given age. We must respect the facts, and the facts merely
confirm the diagnosis we have already made. Many of the
phenomena of the fifteenth century were no longer Catholic
in the full sense of the word.

Humanism is by far the best illustration of the dialectic
tension, the spirit of disquiet and unending search for renewal which characterized the period. It is simply impossible to describe humanism in a few paragraphs; we will try
merely to give a general indication of its nature.

In itself humanism was a transformation, a break with
old ways, an ecstatic experience. With seeming confidence
it preached the gospel of world renewal, yet feared the
specter of world destruction. It was sated with the past, felt
superior to it in a rather conceited way, and consciously
directed all its energies to the future. Its most distinctive

character is well expressed by its name: humanism, the humane, man stands at the center of things. The whole point of view is different from that of the medieval period in which God had the central position. It is a well known fact that this individualistic spirit had made itself felt even in the High Middle Ages and the process can be studied in the laicized piety of the allegories of Gottfried of Strassburg (who died before 1220). In his book *Welt als Geschichte* (1941), Jost Trier has described the allegories as a massive attempt to break down the whole scale of values of Christian chivalry. The same spirit can be observed in the presence of somewhat less than reverent carvings in the vicinity of the altar in the Naumburg Cathedral.

Yet these were merely isolated tendencies. In the age of humanism they assume a rôle so important that individualism must be recognized as one of the essential characteristics of the whole movement. The medieval period is not yet over; many of its elements are to be found in humanism. It does not reflect the individualistic and subjectivistic approach alone, but one would not expect to find them in all their clarity and purity at the beginnings of a movement. Nevertheless, it is the appearance of new ideas that mold the world outlook of a coming age that is of critical importance.

The proper distinctive element in humanism was its orientation not toward God but toward man and this world. This appears not in the sense of the balanced medieval synthesis, exemplified by the writings of Thomas Aquinas, but rather of a new, wholly one-sided development which upset all balance and destroyed the synthesis. That this one-sided development was tempered in the Baroque period and the inevitable consequences were delayed, complicates the picture. But the seed had been planted to flower during the Enlightenment. Humanism was the foundation on which the superstructure of the Enlightenment was built; not that humanism alone was responsible, but it was an important factor.

The same thing is true concerning the Reformation. In a very immediate sense, humanism was a cause of the Reformation. Jedin has said that the Reformation sounded the death knell of humanism before it had developed to full maturity, but it seems rather that, if the tumultuous events of the religious revolt had not revealed the dangers implicit in humanism, men like Erasmus would never have paused to assess the possible evil effects of their mocking criticisms.

In humanism, man occupies the center of the stage; the age of subjectivism and anthropocentrism was dawning; man was soon to become the measure of things. The concept of *virtus* occupied a central place in the thought of the times, and the theme of human dignity was repeated with infinite variation. Note that the "dignity of man" here means something quite different from that mentioned in the prayer said at the preparation of the chalice during Mass. Humanism asserts that God gave man the power to utterly transform himself.

The humanistic theme of the dignity of man immediately brings to mind St. Augustine, the first "modern man." In the seventeenth chapter of the tenth book of the *Confessions* he asks: "My God, what am I? What is the real nature of this life of mine? My life is a complex thing of many facets, endowed with tremendous powers and an almost unlimited field of activity." This seems to be similar to the humanistic view, but the whole tone of the humanistic position is utterly different from that of Augustine whose consciousness is permeated by a spirit of faith.

Augustine means exactly what Leo the Great meant when
he directed his words to men precisely as Christians: "O
Christian, know your worth; you have become a partaker
in the divine nature."

The problem is complex. For the individual as for society, a critical juncture is reached when either becomes aware
of its particular endowments and values and turns an interested gaze on itself. This is the moment when the elements
that were enveloped in the protective aura of the subcon-
scious are exposed to the light of day. With the almost
ecstatic awakening of man brought about by humanism, and
an incessant and exaggerated emphasis on the dignity of
man, it was almost inevitable that St. Paul's warning would
be neglected: "Now we who are strong ought to bear the
infirmities of the weak and not strive to please ourselves"
(Romans 15:1).

The following words are typical of the whole humanistic movement: "Man, you alone of all creatures are unlimited; you are not of heaven, not of earth, not mortal, not
immortal; you are master of your fate; you are free to sink
to the lowest depths and free to rise to the heights of divinity; it is man's greatest good fortune that he may be
whatever he desires to be."

These are the words not only of a Christian, but of an
heroic Christian, Count Pico della Mirandola, who even in
his youth forsook the promises of a brilliant career in the
world and turned to a life of penance and poverty with his
crucified Lord. No less a figure than Savonarola preached
his funeral oration, though it must be admitted that he had
fault to find with certain aspects of the Count's life. At the
same time it is hard to see in these words the expression of
a truly Christian view of things; rather they indicate the
great danger always lurking in unrestrained praise of man's

natural powers. Here we have a picture of man lost in ad-
miration of himself. How often we find in della Mirandola
the dangerous Socratic error of which the humanists were
so fond, the eager evasion of ethical and religious responsibility, by the thesis that the natural excellence of man's
own nature together with his artistic and scientific achievements were the key to inner purification. Time and time
again man's spiritual perfection was equated with rational
pagan morality, and in a way which smacked dangerously
of relativism. It was imagined that pagan man and Christian man were striving for essentially the same truth. The
dangers inherent in the ancient idea of the *logos spermatikos* are once more apparent here. Yet these are the words
of a man who was a true son of the Church. In his case,
Christian heroism stood in the way of the evil effects of this
worldly and all too human view. We know, however, that
the fifteenth century was far from being an age of heroes.
What were the ordinary people of the day who went with
the current of the times to make out of such ideas after they
became literary common places?

Are we then to describe humanism as a neo-pagan
movement? By no means! The whole structure of humanism was erected by Christians. Its sources were Christian
ideas of rebirth and regeneration through the waters of
baptism and a new order inaugurated by the descent of the
Holy Ghost. Furthermore, a fine and genuine humanism
developed during the Late Middle Ages in the Low Countries and restricted itself almost entirely to the pedagogical
sphere. I know as well that in our own day any number
of individuals have found in Christianity the inspiration for
their humanistic ideals.

Humanism as such was not pagan, although individuals
and groups of humanists spoke and acted as though it were,

but it did bear the imprint of a dangerous intellectual,
moral, and, if I may use the expression, religious secular-
ism. We simply miss the point at issue by asserting that
many elements of the Christian heritage lived on in humanism; we simply cannot grasp intellectual movements and
their influence on the human spirit by analyzing their elements statically. We can penetrate their mystery only by
searching for truly dynamic factors and tendencies that sustained and nourished the movement. We must ask what
will the movement become after the dialectical process has
exhausted all its possibilities and reached full development.
When we ask this question of humanism, the answer is simple and quite discouraging for us as Catholics: the movement resulted in the popes of the Renaissance in their
Renaissance culture. We can see that the movement termi-
nated not in a renewal of the world in Christ, but in a
dangerous secularization of the Christian elements of that
world.

Solutions in accord with Christian ideals exemplified
by St. Thomas More and *humanisme dévot* pose a special
problem, but leave our main thesis untouched.

Another essential aspect of humanism was a tendency
to attack all that the immediate past represented. To be
sure, humanism was much more than a break with the medieval past; in fact, humanism, like the Renaissance in
North Italy, had deep medieval roots. We have only to think
of Dante, Petrarch, and the early German humanists to
realize this. Nevertheless, humanism was above all a rupture with the past, a conscious and critical rejection of the
immediately preceding era.

Humanism devoted much effort to criticizing all aspects
of the Church, especially monasticism and scholasticism.

The humanists had little appreciation of the vital concept of the spiritual life, the intellectual culture and the inner dynamism of the medieval period which they felt were qualities of their own time. Frequently they were right.

In many ways, scholasticism had brought this criticism on itself by undergoing developments similar to those that we discussed regarding political tendencies of the Curia. Forms of expression conditioned by purely temporal factors were confused with a content that ought to have enduring value: scholastics sometimes acted as though their theological theories were identical with the deposit of faith. The unfortunate result was that, in attacking the one, humanism attacked the other also. Undeniably the humanists' critique of scholasticism in the fifteenth century was to a great extent justified, since the whole tone of late medieval scholasticism did not do much to reveal the riches of the faith.

It may be objected that none of this was too serious because humanism was essentially an aristocratic movement that affected only the upper strata of society. First of all, this is only partially true, for powerful movements have an effect far beyond the circle of those who consciously accept their principles; their influence permeates society through any number of channels. From the strictly religious and theological viewpoint, this influence spread to the new forms that devotional life took at the time. A relatively small group of humanists became spokesmen for society as a whole. In Germany, this group happened to be the most radical one, the humanists of Erfurt. Among these the criticism of the Church was most subversive and gradually passed over into the sphere of dogma. Far from the spirit of the sacramental Roman Church, Erfurt humanists were inspired to a great extent by a deep hatred of the Church and

her priests; their criticism of monasticism was little more
than a criticism of the religious ideal itself and these spokesmen lived practically like pagans.

This is of great significance for an understanding of
future developments in the Church, for ideas appeared that
tended toward an erroneous interpretation of the essence
of Christianity. In proof of this, we need only note the fact
that the circles in which these ideas were prevalent were
also sharply opposed to the doctrines on prayer and sacrifice accepted by the Church.

Secondly, many of these ideas were Stoic in origin. In
an earlier age, the apologetical writers of the second century lost sight of the person and work of the Savior to the
extent of viewing monotheism as the essential element in
Christianity. However, they selected this point for tactical
reasons; they did not impose a heterodox system on Christianity. The case was quite different with the Erfurt school,
which was in a true sense a precursor of the Enlightenment.
Christianity is monotheistic, but the definition is false if
formulated as it has been done in recent years: monotheism
is Christianity. When this is done, Christianity is deprived
of a distinctive and indispensable element—Jesus Christ.
When this is done, all the higher religions of the world become quite similar; dogma is no longer a value and the
danger of relativism is imminent.

Through its contact with antiquity, humanism emphasized the natural powers of man, particularly the power of
his will. We have already discussed the principal aspects of
this view. As in the case of a one-sided monotheism, this
new approach was incapable of grasping the real nature of
salvation, and the function of grace in the process of salvation was neglected. Both points of view showed dangerous
tendencies to interpret Christianity in a moralistic sense, so

that humanism became a force that tended to destroy Christianity. In all of these developments we find the isolated "superior morality" of the synoptic Gospels, interpreted in a Stoic sense; in addition, this concept, so important in the Bible's message, was stripped of its religious overtones and its absolute value.

Thus this small radical group of humanists succeeded in spreading its influence far and wide. From a dispute with Reuchlin over Jewish theology immediately before and during the outbreak of the Reformation, the notorious *Dunkelmännerbriefe* had their origin. Witty, ironical, often coarse and malicious, but always appealing to the reader in clever ways, these lying and slanderous little pamphlets succeeded in persuading people at large that the humanists alone were really modern, while all others were simply out of date.

In general the theology of the humanists was not profound; as a whole it cannot compare with scholasticism. Even the Erfurt school offered no real competition. Yet the decline of scholasticism proved that, though truth is timeless and independent of the form in which it is expressed, its influence is profoundly affected by its form. The truth must nourish those who hear it; it is extremely important that it be presented in a vital way. If formulated in a tiresome and boring way, its very profundity will work against it.

The objection might be raised that the success of the humanists, a literary victory for a few critics and laymen who lived in pagan style, and the influence of the Erfurt school would be short-lived. That they could exert lasting influence seems improbable. Yet they did, for their work was continued to a great extent by a man whose life testifies to the power inherent in the humanistic revival—Desiderius Erasmus of Rotterdam.

I have no intention of calling Erasmus a bohemian. I
do not assert that he belonged to the circle of the Erfurt humanists. We must be careful to make the right distinctions
lest we misunderstand and judge Erasmus wrongly. I hope
to escape the wrath of Erasmus's admirers by making clear
that I believe he was unexcelled in scholarship, especially
philology. As one of the most cultured and clever men of
his day, he achieved remarkable results in the development
of scientific pedagogical methods. Erasmus was most renowned in all of these fields for achievements that are simply amazing to anyone with any acquaintance with them
at all.

We, however, are presently interested in Erasmus the
theologian. It is legitimate to ask whether his influence on
religion and the Church was a constructive or destructive
one—even radically destructive; whether his criticism of
the Church produced any good or rather threatened its very
existence. Did Erasmus possess the fullness of the Christian
faith? Was he truly a religious influence in his understanding of the theology of the Cross? Are we not forced to say
that he tended to make out of Christianity a religion of
culture or even a cultural morality?

We can merely indicate one or two possible answers
to these difficult questions. To the question What is the
fundamental message of our Lord's preaching? the synoptic
Gospels furnish the answer: Christ came to preach a higher
and more internal morality, the adoration of God in spirit
and truth. He came in order to take the external formalism
out of religion. If that is true, then Erasmus ranks as one
of the greatest Christians. Throughout his whole life, with
tremendous energy, he devoted all of his genius to the interiorization of Christendom and the Christian spirit, to
freeing religion from the material and the external. We

certainly must not overlook how easily the "adoration in spirit and truth" of the New Testament can be given a spiritualistic misinterpretation. The perennial danger faced by Christian doctrine of falling victim to a purely human process of sublimation is evident here. In ever-increasing measure from the time of the Reformation, this has constituted a threat to the faith so that in the Enlightenment it attacked the essential elements of Christianity. We cannot say that Erasmus escaped this danger entirely; his philosophy of the Christian is deficient in a number of ways. Erasmus was most deeply interested in all the phenomena of religion, but was he a religious man in the sense of the theologian whose main concerns are God, the Church, and Christian holiness? This is not merely desirable but a matter of strict necessity?

We must be as prudent as possible in passing judgment. Erasmus is not an easy man to understand. Because he was an original thinker, he forged a new vocabulary to express his novel insights; consequently, his terminology at times lacks precision. His expressions are difficult to pinpoint and limit to a definite meaning; he is forever conscious of the infinite variety found in concrete situations. In this he is an important precursor of the modern age. There is another element that complicates the interpretation: a definite, rather smug, sceptical irony, well aware of the limitations of this much-touted thing called intellect and keenly aware of the mental mediocrity of mankind. How serious is Erasmus when he criticizes? Is he merely toying with his readers? A recent reviewer, writing of the *Memoirs* of the early life of Churchill, expressed an interesting view: "The English talent for understatement—the art of toning down everything and putting it in a far less serious light than is really intended—is used by Churchill to such an extent that a

European reader must find the result somewhat frivolous."
Perhaps this also explains much about Erasmus. We hope
so. Yet we are forced to repeat the question: Was Erasmus
religious, a Christian in the full and complete sense of the
word?

Erasmus had no desire to break away from the Church
and he never did. After a long period of fence-straddling,
he even rose to defend its doctrines against Luther, as we
shall see. But in the case of a priest, monk, or theological
writer, you cannot regard merely staying in the Church as
the measure of profound Catholic spirit. Concerning his
recognition of the Catholic doctrines of grace, expressed
in sceptical enough formulas, we must remember that this,
coming as it did in 1524, was not without some self-interest.
Erasmus had no desire for martyrdom; thus his burning
concern of the moment was to avoid the anathemas proclaimed against the heretics.

Was Erasmus essentially a religious man in the sense
that Christianity demands? To compose prayers, to demand
adoration "in spirit and truth," to condemn external formalism in witty and sarcastic fashion is not the same as to have
one's prayer and life inspired and sustained by faith. One
belongs to the order of good and not so good intentions; the
other belongs to the real order.

Of course, if we were to do justice to Erasmus, we would
have to emphasize his positive contributions to the Church
far more than it is possible in just a few lines. We must
emphasize that a Saint like Thomas More was a close friend
of Erasmus; so was the martyred Bishop, John Fisher.
Later, men whose Christianity was deeply influenced by
the sacraments, dogma and awareness of the nature of the
Church (as was the case with the counter-reformer, Cardinal Hosius) were among the greatest admirers of Eras-

mus. This is precisely why we have to underline our thesis on the negative contributions of Erasmus. In addition, an analysis of the history of ideas is never interested in finding the Christian heritage of a man or a movement in as limited a form as possible. The greater the extent to which this heritage is possessed, the better, for St. Paul's statement is always true: *"dummodo Christus praedicetur."*

But this can't be the last word in the serious examination we are making here. Let's take the problem where it is most difficult: Thomas More, a Saint and a very close and intimate friend of Erasmus, defended his *In Praise of Folly*. First of all, the judgment of a Saint cannot change the facts, but it may help us to realize more clearly the negative nature of Erasmus's contribution. Secondly, it was one of the most characteristic qualities of Thomas More that he never interfered in the affairs of others and refrained from saying anything that would harm a friendship unless it involved a vital matter of conscience. When this point was reached, he took a definite stand and took it heroically. The story of the trial that led to his beheading is eloquent testimony of this. Thus the Saint could cultivate the intimate friendship of Erasmus, whose renowned achievements in the world of scholarship provided a source of common interest, without being troubled in the least by the profound difference in their religious points of view. That this profound difference did exist is evidenced by the fact that for all his humanism More never lost sight of the crippling effect of original sin on human nature. This was no mere theoretical concern. More lived according to this conviction. He practiced penance; he obeyed the laws of the Church on fasting; the Church, the Mass and the sacraments were the source of his spiritual life—in this he was unlike Erasmus, the monk and priest.

We still must mention an extremely significant contribution, much to Erasmus's credit: his work on the Greek New Testament that culminated in the publication of the Greek text, an epoch-making achievement. Through this work, part of a great intellectual movement and an expression of its most vital dynamism, the word of God in its genuine original form, in its entirety and with all its nuances of meaning preserved intact, was opened up as a source of prayer and theological study. It was in a sense returned to its own age, brought nearer to its time than had been the case since Christian antiquity. And with this, the inexhaustible riches of the Bible, the unique prophetic and religious message of the New Testament, were opened up once more to the reflection of the Christian spirit. The Bible could once more be understood in its proper setting; it could be read and felt, as Erasmus said, as though it had been written but yesterday. These were the Holy Scriptures, as he put it in his Prologue to the New Testament addressed to Leo X, "in which the Word of Heaven which came to us once from the bosom of the Father, still lives, breathes, acts, and speaks to us with all his divine power and condescension."

Unfortunately, even here we cannot overlook a negative element. In his presentation of the text and his important introduction concerning method, in spite of his express and repeated recognition of the teaching office of the Church, in practice, we meet only an individual scholar in place of the magisterium. From this point of view, Erasmus's work on the New Testament prepared the way for Luther far more than did the Greek text itself, which Luther was able to master to a limited extent only. (The most recent studies indicate that in making his translation, Luther made far more use of the old Latin Vulgate text.) Still, let us

remember what has been said to Erasmus's credit and not
lose sight of it. Despite all of this his contribution was de-
cidedly negative.

The first point to be made in this regard is the one
repeatedly emphasized by Huizinga, the greatest authority
on the humanistic period. He regards Erasmus as the great
master of ambiguous expression. It is not merely difficult
to find what Erasmus meant exactly; the real difficulty is
that there is no exact meaning there. In this Erasmus is a
good example of the theological confusion of the day. In
his important treatise on free will, where he defends the
doctrine of the Church against innovators, he makes no
attempt to distinguish the essential from the non-essential;
he seems to be willing to treat the entire matter as a somewhat remote and theoretical disputation. Deep down he is
unwilling to commit himself and his ideas to the strife of
the marketplace and consequently fears that this may happen. Dear to his heart and a great consolation to him is a
faith that is a stranger to the sword which the Lord brought
(Matt. 10:34).

The time has now come to elaborate our ideas on the
essential characteristics of Christianity. It is proper to the
Christian faith, essential, one might say, that its truth must
be a two-edged sword. Christianity demands that its ad-
herents make a definitive commitment; this involves the
whole man. The "independent" man is the antithesis of the
Christian. In this respect, Erasmus is profoundly unchristian. Even when Erasmus speaks of more important aspects
of Christian doctrine and discipline, he speaks in a sceptical
way, as though it doesn't really matter. He has a strong
tendency to *adogmatism*. He has no more concept of dogma
as an exact statement of Christian teaching than did the
men of the Enlightenment or modern liberal Protestants.

No one recognized this fact more clearly and made more of it than Luther in the First Preface to his work *Vom geknechteten Willen*. What this indifference to dogma means is certainly clear to us today, the heirs of four hundred years of religious development after the Reformation. We understand better than any generation before us that adogmatism must bear the blame for the weakening of Christianity and the dilution of its teaching throughout recent centuries.

We have already made clear how necessary it is for healthy theological thought to be connected to the sacramental life of the Church. We traced the decline of a certain type of late medieval theology to the lack of this connection. Erasmus is by far the most important example in the history of the Church for a type of theology that has lost its roots in the sacramental life of the Church. Erasmus was a priest, but just as he celebrated Mass on only the rarest occassions, he died without the sacraments.

Erasmus made many contributions to the literature of his day in the field of religion and the spiritual life. Unfortunately even his works of piety affected his readers as being something less than religious. Ignatius of Loyola was quite right when he said that some of the passages of the *Enchiridion* had a chilling effect on him. Erasmus confused religion and culture far too often for us to be able to say that his thought was rooted in the faith in the true sense of the word.

Furthermore, Erasmus tended to take a dangerously over-spiritualized view of the Church. Though he did not deny the reality of grace and talked of the insufficiency of man despite his free will in a most orthodox manner, he did preach Christianity primarily as morality. In the practical order, he so emphasized man's own powers of intellect and will that he came dangerously close to moralism.

Erasmus, with his sensitive reactions, active mind, and gifts of lively expression cannot be judged from one or two phrases. Quoting a sentence or two from his works is no guarantee that they adequately represent the real convictions of the man; to understand Erasmus, we must consider all that they are, all that they say, and all that they do. Without doubt Erasmus had strong leanings in the direction of the Socratic error that knowledge was the same as virtue and Christian purification. To quote just one of many possible passages, he says in the *Antibarbari:* "What is Christian charity without knowledge? It is a ship without a rudder." This is just the opposite of St. Paul's doctrine (1 Cor. 13). The Socratic error is nothing but exaggerated trust in the human spirit, translated into the process of justification; it is nothing more than moralism.

This point is worthy of emphasis: In his disputation on freedom of will, any number of times we are told in the most orthodox fashion, at times quite emphatically, that all of man's powers and gifts come from God, that man must beware of pride and self-sufficiency, that everything a man can do with his intellect and will belongs to God (*Diatribe*, 75). But for one thing, this *Diatribe* was written by Erasmus as a proof of his orthodoxy, and secondly, the picture of man which Erasmus gives us in his pedagogical and moral tracts, in his letters and by his example, is more to the point. The answer is not too encouraging. At the very least we are forced to assert that he did not draw the practical consequences from his statements that attribute everything to God and His Grace.

We must say something more on the adogmatism mentioned before. If, as Erasmus thought, dogma is something superfluous; if, as he thought, the doctrine of Christianity could and should be restricted to a few general points, Erasmus was quite near the erroneous interpretation which would equate Christianity with monotheism. When this is done, Christianity becomes indistinguishable from the other higher religions and thus, relativism is just around the corner.

If all this is true, then we have to agree that Erasmus constituted a grave threat to the Church—not because of the frequently frivolous and mocking criticism he directed at it, but because of his adogmatism, moralism, and relativism.

The pope at the time was the humanist Leo X who had a great regard for Erasmus and was quite unaware of the threat which the latter constituted for the Church. Thus we find the papal delegate Alexander writing from the Diet of Worms in 1521: "For heaven's sake, don't send us any more privileges for Erasmus. The man is doing far more harm than Luther ever can." Luther was precisely the one who recognized and rejected the danger from the quarter of the humanists. With all the violence of his characteristically one-sided approach, Luther turned from the cultural morality he found in the humanists to the religion of faith as he found it in St. Paul.

The question provoked by all these developments is this: Precisely what were the strong and weak points of the Church as it entered the era of the Reformation? It is difficult to give an exact answer to this question, since there are so many facets to the problem. One answer is no sooner given than it must be modified and restricted; distressing events must always be counterbalanced by the more encouraging ones. In the realm of the spiritual it is extremely difficult to give an exact account of the forces and factors involved. How different was the situation in various regions. Finally it is important to recall that religious life had by no means reached the state of decadence once attributed to it. Many more positive factors were at work than men were willing to admit previously.

Nevertheless, we have to ask what distinctively characterized that age, whether it was essentially strong from the religious point of view, or noteworthy for various forms of abuses. (This will be a key word in our discussion.) In recent years, many have considered this an overworked thesis. I do not by any means agree. There is question of the existence or non-existence of an essential Christian element in the Church. All we have to do is to be extremely clear about what we mean by abuses.

When we speak of abuses in the Church, many people immediately begin to think of the "bad" popes, the scandals of the rule of Alexander VI and many other similar examples. Of course these are important. For the personal sanctity of the clergy it is extremely significant whether or not this type of thing happens frequently in the Church, but it is not of critical importance. Religious and moral collapse do not decide these issues but the correct or incorrect interpretation of the essential elements of Christianity.

Inquiries concerning the subjective guilt of the popes, bishops, or the lower clergy are useless. It is to the point to ask about the objective strength of the Church. We are interested in the objective causes of difficulties in the Church and to what extent they became historically important factors. We ask whether the collapse which came was merely a chance event or due to structural flaws in the Church of the fifteenth century. We will see that this was by no means a question of chance but rather of important

structural defects, for example, the influence of politics in
the religious sphere and the far too important place which
the economic element (benefices) had won in the organization of the Church. We are fully aware that political
interests of the secular powers, the pride and pleasure-seek-
ing of large numbers of the laity had their part to play as
well; if anything, this makes the picture even darker. Otherwise, we would imply that there is no such thing as a sick
man, but only sick microbes which destroy healthy organ-
isms. The precise question is whether or not the Church had
enough inner strength to exclude those microbes and pre-
vent them from infecting her.

In other words, to what extent in those days did men have
a genuine idea of the Church, the priesthood, and monasticism? To what extent was the real pastoral care being exercised? Were the positive factors in the situation creative
or exhausted? Was the spiritual life a truly vital reality or
merely an external set of conventions?

We have to avoid another misunderstanding if we are to
study the situation honestly and sincerely. We can't regard
the bare minimum of orthodoxy as enough when we weigh
the factors which influenced the Church in the Reformation
period. Negative correctness, the lack of mistakes, is not a
Christian category but a superficial one. Christianity is
power and truth; it is a category which embraces what is
within man and most essential to his nature.

One more prenote. Abuses in the late medieval period
are frequently referred to as "Roman." We will soon see
that the abuses in which we are interested were all too prevalent at Rome. Yet, fundamentally, the mistakes made were
not of Roman origin. Everything that the Reformation objected to as formalism, hypocrisy, time-serving, and even
idolatry in the Roman Church, in other words, the over-

working of the merit concept in questions of moral and religious guilt, were all of German origin. The reward concept, *do ut des* as a fundamental moral attitude, stemmed from pre-Christian Germanic concepts in the religious or juridical order and from the peculiar character of the early missionary activity among the Germanic tribes. Overemphasis on the reward idea and too infrequent approach to the sacraments was of thoroughly Germanic origin. The rather surprising result is that when Luther revolted in the name of his German and Christian consciousness against "Roman" abuses, he was actually revolting against decadent practices which were German in origin and for which Germans must bear the blame.

We turn now to the concrete situation at various levels of the Church. The first point to note is the extreme secularization of the Roman Curia. To see this in all its importance we must examine not the papacy of Alexander VI but of Julius II and more so of Leo X. Pope Leo X was not open to charges of immorality, but in him we can recognize a representative of the thoroughly worldly type of thinking present in the Curia and simply accepted by all as proper. All we need do is recall the grand entry of Leo X into the city of Rome. Theoretically this event took place in a procession of the Blessed Sacrament; actually the Blessed Sacrament did not hold the center of the stage. The real attraction was the splendid spectacle of the cardinals, their retinues and the magnificently attired Pope himself. As he rode through the triumphal arches, decorated with nude statues, the impression created justified the popular appraisal of the three successive popes, Alexander VI, Julius II, and Leo X: "First Venus held sway, then Mars, and now Pallas Athena."

This was a suitable beginning for a pontificate for which

the Pope had chosen the motto: "Let us enjoy the Papacy, for God has given it to us."

In this milieu we can, of course, find any number of examples to show the subchristian if not unchristian way of life at the center of Christendom. Whether we recall that Erasmus was able to hear in the Pope's own chapel on Good Friday an ostentatious piece of humanistic oratory in which Our Lord and His Passion were not even mentioned, while the speaker displayed his learning and the glories of pagan antiquity; or whether we note that papal ambassadors were merely diplomats who operated solely in a diplomatic, not a religious context, even when purely religious matters were involved (as Alexander at the Diet of Worms in 1521), no one was in the least surprised at this way of acting; the picture of profound secularization in the holy places remains the same.

In addition we can recall the evils that had characterized the power complex of the Roman Curia since the time of Avignon: arbitrariness, the multiplication of ways of conferring spiritual favors, simony, wealth, and hedonistic existence, whether manifested in crude or refined forms.

It is not surprising, but rather quite logical that the Curia had no concept of the basically religious problems that were to provoke the Reformation. This is manifest in the fact that it was in this worldly milieu that that traffic began which immediately triggered Luther's revolt. When Albrecht of Brandenburg, who at the age of twenty-five already had two bishoprics to his credit plus a monastery, was elected Archbishop of Mainz, he wished to keep control of all three. Known as a *cumulus,* this was expressly forbidden by Church law. The tithes which were to be sent to Rome from Mainz in confirmation of the appointment came to 14,000 gold guilders. The Papal Curia itself now made the novel suggestion that it would be possible for Albrecht to keep all three bishoprics by sending to Rome another 10,000 gold guilders. Including some important tips, the new Archbishop ended up sending some 25,000 gold guilders to Rome, which he had borrowed from the banking house of Fugger. In order to facilitate his repayment of the loan, Rome commissioned Albrecht with the preaching of the indulgence for the rebuilding of St. Peter's in the districts of Mainz and Brandenburg, with the stipulation that the proceeds should be split three ways—one third to the Curia, one third to Albrecht, and one third to the House of Fugger.

This was the background of the preaching of the indulgence by Tetzel which soon began; the preaching was burdened from the start with the "fire-sale" tone of the Briefs which proclaimed the indulgence and with the fact that the indulgences themselves were practically being sold. There is little doubt that Tetzel's preaching was well summed up in the phrase, "a coin in the box opens heaven to your soul," and there is no doubt either that the deal between Albrecht and the Curia as well as the lively trade in indulgences would have been condemned as the worst type of simony in the early Church.

It is obvious enough that in those times the Curia had little interest in pastoral problems, prayer and the sacraments, and that the struggle against the coming Reformation was to be conducted with anything but religious weapons.

If some feel that the picture could not be as black as I have painted it, I would point to the weighty judgment pronounced by the most religious-minded pope of the period, Adrian VI of Utrecht, the last German pope. What he said comes down to this: So widespread are the sins of the Curia, that those who run it are no longer aware of the foul stench. Adrian had been trained in the humanist tradition, and it might be thought that he had exaggerated a bit because of this training. This would be wrong, for when it came to religious matters, Adrian VI was soberly serious. He was acquainted with world affairs, for he once had been a tutor of Charles V; he knew the meaning of responsibility and showed it. He knew what he was doing when he instructed Chierigati, his legate to the Diet of Nuremberg in 1522, "You are to say (publicly!) that everything wrong with the Church is due to the sins of her priests and, above all, to the papal court."

This condemnation of religious collapse at the very heart of Christendom is extremely important, especially if viewed from the standpoint of the doctrine of the Communion of Saints, so essential for the life of the Church. The Church is essentially a unity; the weakness of one member is the weakness of all. This remains a point of prime importance even apart from the naturally pernicious effects of bad example by those who should have been channels of grace and should have given the best example.

We should now study the various levels of the teaching and ruling Church, the cardinals, bishops, and the clergy. Divided by such an unfortunate chasm from the hierarchy, the lower clergy became a spiritual proletariat in the worst sense of the word. In summary, we can say that at every level what really characterized the Church was not an esteem of religious values, but just the opposite state.

The general situation was such that the Church seemed to be the property of the clergy, designed to help them lead the good life, to provide money and pleasure. The concern for money dominated the thoughts and plans of the Curia as well as the cardinals, bishops, pastors, abbots, and on

down the line. This can be discerned in the pursuit after
benefices, the practice of leaving pastoral concerns to
poorly paid substitutes, who became hirelings to whom the
sheep did not belong (John 10:12). This practice along
with the accompanying phenomenon of non-residence were
both unbelievably widespread. The intermingling of the material and the spiritual, the religious and economic spheres,
so characteristic of the Middle Ages exhibited tremendous
dangers to the constitution of a genuine interior Christian
spirit. The bad effects of this confusion were to last, despite
the essential reforms effected by Trent, up to the time of
the French Revolution when the confusion came at last to
an end.

The situation in the monasteries is worthy of special
mention. The more we come to know of the history of individual areas, the more we realize that the earlier universal
condemnation of the monasteries and the indiscriminate
charge of universal immorality was a grievous calumny.
Even apart from the important reform movements we have
to realize that among the unreformed monasteries, a far
greater number were morally sound than was heretofore
suspected.

It remains true, however, that throughout the episcopacy
and in the monasteries, the nobility was definitely in control. It remains true that by the practice of the sale of
abbacies and the multiplication of privileges by Rome in
favor of monasteries or individuals belonging to them (e.g.,
permission to live outside the cloister, permission to possess
private property, exemption of the monastery from diocesan jurisdiction) the rules of religious orders were ren-
dered so meaningless that the idea of religious life became
devoid of content. Greater damage was done by the spirit
of competition between the orders. Few creative elements

were active at the time; in their place reigned lassitude, not only in spiritual and intellectual pursuits, but in the management of the properties necessary for the well-being of the monasteries and abbeys.

Here and there at different levels of the Church Christian life was lived authentically. Yet, as we have already mentioned, this is quite irrelevant to the question of whether or not the Church as a whole was in good shape or not. It does not eliminate the powerful, destructive influences which we have already examined in our study of the chain of causes that led to the Reformation: the destruction of medieval unity, widespread discontent with conditions in the Church, theological confusion, the harmful elements in humanism, and finally, the profound collapse of religious life, particularly in the Roman Curia and among the higher clergy in general. In recent years the mistake has often been made of regarding a quite average level of Christian life in a particular diocese as an encouraging sign for the period, but this conclusion is false. Mediocrity in a given diocese in the midst of a world where sanctity stands in high esteem is tolerable, but when the Christian people are no longer living an exemplary and even heroic life of faith, when large areas of Christendom have come to be profoundly unchristian, then mediocrity is no longer encouraging or even tolerable. Such a diocese cannot resist the overwhelming influence of the surrounding milieu.

Is the picture I have painted too one-sided? I did say that any number of distinctions must be made, that many positive elements existed in the situation which should be taken into account. Europe as a whole was a vast and confusing mosaic of mediocrity, total religious ruin, or true religious vitality, but the impression we are left with is in accordance with the facts we have given; unfortunately that was the real situation. It only remains for Catholics to pronounce their *mea culpa*.

The whole difficulty in describing the state of affairs is first apparent when we turn to the question of popular religious life. What are genuinely Christian elements in this complex mass of various forms of piety? We are faced with a confusion of externalism and interiority, solid devotion to the Church and overspiritualized piety, genuine faith and abject superstition.

Next we must find out what was the rôle of each of these healthy and unhealthy symptoms in bringing about the Reformation.

We can point to a great increase in manifestations of piety within the Church: massive and imposing structures, new foundations that would have been impossible without the concerted action of many vital forces and without the expenditure of a good deal of money and labor. Unfortunately this is not a conclusive proof for the existence of the genuine Christian spirit. Much is explained by the spirit of pride and competition.

The low estate of popular sacramental life was a bad sign; from many different countries indications of popular ignorance in matters of religion can be adduced. It is true that the Church made great efforts to educate her children, through the stained glass windows in the Church, illustrated Bibles and so on, but the results were far from satisfying. Popular piety was far too frequently nothing but moralism or crass formalism that in practice degenerated into hypocrisy and superstition. Much of this was due to the selfish, money-centered view of their profession taken by many of the clergy—Session 25 of the Council of Trent was to detail the harmful effects of this attitude on the souls entrusted to their care.

All of these developments took place in a context of great devotion to the Church and her doctrine. Here again we see the fifteenth century as a century of violent contrasts. It was of decisive importance that this flowering of a spirit of loyalty to the Church went hand in hand with strong popular discontent with the clergy. W. P. Fuchs has described the situation in these terms: "The Church was a despised, moneyed power, which through its system of taxation held the common man in its claws." The behavior of the tenant farmers who rose against the monks is proof enough of this.

The lax life led by many clerics had a bad effect on the picture the faithful formed of the Church. There are any number of complaints on record against the public concubinage of priests. But we also find the surprising phenomenon of priests who, though they lived in concubinage, were much esteemed by their people, as many of them were good pastors, thoroughly devoted to the spiritual progress of their flocks.

We will not delay long in giving examples of the crass and obvious formalism of the day: decadent practices in granting indulgences, the exaggerated honor accorded relics, the pilgrimage craze, the disproportionate place given to the veneration of the saints—all constituted a dangerous development. These factors played an important rôle in the movement away from the Church and the spirit of the Christian life. The most pernicious feature was the fact that the people were not aware of it. They made the faithful susceptible to the appeal of any form of radical movement; but this seems so well known that this brief outline sketch will suffice.

We prefer to examine the other side of the coin. Religious piety was far more sound among the people than the clergy. Two indications of this are still available to us: the pious literature of the day and Christian art.

In the category of edifying literature we find a great number of prayer books, books on confession, explanations of the Mass, books to prepare for a good death, and the body of literature of the *devotio moderna* school. In all of them love, not fear, is given as the motive of contrition; emphasis is put not on man's but God's part in the process of salvation, and the Crucified Lord is the very heart of this devotion.

As a single example, I would mention a book I trust all are acquainted with: *The Following of Christ* by Thomas à Kempis. This work was intended primarily for religious; thus the intellectual and religious world from which it was created offers certain problems that are unknown to those who make use of the book for spiritual reading in these times. A certain element of moralism is implicit in the piety it proposes, but on the whole this form of piety builds on the strong foundations, not of formalism, but of a genuine Christian spirit. Its prayer is not directed to a multitude of saints whose aid is sought for every little crisis. It is centered on our Lord and His sacraments. The task of all Christians is to lose themselves in Him. There is no hypocrisy here. Even the dangerous principle of Ockhamistic theology: "If a man does what he can, God will not deny His grace," is used in the *Following of Christ* to foster the knowledge and realization that it is only God who works and that only His grace can accomplish anything in us.

The story is clearer when we look at the Christian art of the period. It was a time of true genius, as Pinder remarked, the time of Dürer, Grünwald, Riemenschneider and many others. The work of all of these men was religious to the core. The lack of mere formalism in their works is evidenced by the high artistic quality of their art. On a deeper level, the true Christian interior spirit of the artists, their personal appropriation of Christian truth, speaks to us from any number of their works. To get beyond generalities one would have to examine a number of individual works; this cannot be done here.

The function of this religious art in terms of its future effects is difficult to evaluate; without doubt the deep religious spirit to which it gives testimony could lay the foundation for a religious renewal. We find this verified in fact in both the Reformation and the Catholic Renascence of the next century.

One thing can be definitely asserted: Christian art in this period did not belong to the Reformation because most of it was in existence before the Reformation. Countless references have been made to Dürer's welcoming of Luther and the great interest he showed in Luther's fate on the latter's disappearance from public view immediately after the Diet of Worms. Yet neither should be in the least surprising. Remember that for centuries the cry for a reform in head and members had been rampant in the Church and Dürer was one of those who had high hopes of such a reform; it would, however, be quite arbitrary to see Dürer as one of the reformers. In addition, such a view would ignore all the signs which point to the fact that Dürer led a thoroughgoing Catholic life. To construe Riemenschneider's development as a break with the Church, would, if possible, be even less justified. Grünwald's work was on record before the Reformation came and as such cannot be attributed to it. It is possible that he belonged to those who would have extended the reform even to matters of doctrine; it is true that among his effects were found some writings of

Luther which he had gotten and hence he did know of Luther.

I have noted that this art played a very complex rôle in terms of the future. Actually it also bears signs of the contradictions so characteristic of the medieval period. Riemenschneider is weighed down by the suffering of the world, but looks forward to salvation. Still he is tired; his tendency to suffer in silence, to hold on at all costs, indicates that he was troubled by nagging doubts. In the work of Dürer and Grünwald, the apocalyptic element, portrayed in stark grandeur, is essential. With Grünwald one might even mention a demonic element accompanied by a frightful fear of hell, but he is also the painter of mystic ecstasy. No other ever succeeded in translating the mystical experience to canvas as he did.

Perhaps it is most important to see the dangers implicit in the interiorization of the spiritual life, in itself so estimable and Christian a development. In the case of certain brilliant individuals this interiority led to a subjectivistic isolation from Christendom. When we look at some of the faces in the paintings and see written there an uncertainty, a lack of integration and real fear, this effect is seen more clearly.

To ask the question again—what were the characteristics of popular piety of the time? No single answer can be given. Formerly the tendency would have been to answer that hypocrisy and formalism were rampant everywhere; but that is false. Luther himself bears some responsibility for the fabrication of that fable and in so doing evidenced the uniqueness of his own world view, his tendency toward one-sided exaggeration and the dominant influence of Ockham's theology on him—all working together in ruin-

ous fashion. And yet in the case of so many, we cannot
avoid concluding that they lived as though salvation could
be won by using purely external means.

Why is it that even people who know the history of the
period bristle at the picture we have painted and the conclusions drawn? Part of the explanation is due to their
timid or weak faith, or an exaggeratedly apologetic approach to the period. But there are objective reasons as
well. The data are somewhat ambiguous; we have examples
of the best in theology, culture and liturgy and other
equally impressive examples of the neglect of liturgy, of
deficient religious practice, and of theological confusion.
The facts themselves do not present a unified picture and
hence they are assessed quite differently. This alone explains the violent clash of opinion between the innovators
in the sixteenth century and the Church's theologians in
talking about the situation in Europe and evaluating it.
Their controversy was characterized by exaggerations, a
good deal of crudity and the like, but it is extremely unlikely that the attacks of the reformers on matters that were
open to common knowledge were wholly false. We are
justified in looking on the missals of the day as giving an
adequate picture of the faith of the Church, but we cannot
regard this as an adequate picture of the popular piety of
the time. This is a decisive point and a problem that comes
up again and again in the history of the Church: theology
or some theologians, and with them the Christian consciousness itself, lose contact with the richness and clarity of the
liturgy. The older Catholics of the present generation had a
similar experience in their younger days. In spite of the
religion of grace and the sacraments preserved in the missal, little of it was present in the consciousness and preaching of the clergy or devoted to pastoral work; thus the

practical theology of the pulpit and the confessional was conceived in a juridical framework and smacked of moralism.

After all that has been said, we still don't have an adequate idea of the religious situation of the end of the fifteenth and the beginning of the sixteenth century. Wilhelm Neuss is quite right in his comment: "If, without even suspecting that the Reformation was to come, we were suddenly to come face to face with conditions in the Church around the year 1500, what would we see? A world almost entirely Catholic, rich ecclesiastical life, numerous clergy and monasteries." Despite all that has been said, around 1500 the Church alone was the uncontested leader in all spheres of public and private life. This is an inescapable fact, but what does it prove? Does it negate a single one of the facts we have adduced? By no means! The world of 1500 collapsed with incredible speed. Think of it! Just yesterday, so to speak, the matrons of Nuremberg had brought their daughters to the Convent of the Poor Clares, so that they might lead there a life of perfection as nuns and attain eternal salvation by the safest path. "Today" the same matrons were at the gate with horse and wagon to drag their daughters from the Convent, hurling all kinds of violent abuse about the Convent being the home of the Antichrist and representing nothing but idolatry. Or consider the fact that thousands of monks renounced their vows in a short time, returned to the world, married, and together with Luther, joined the war against the monastic life. Things like this were of such frequent occurrence that it would be an oversimplification to attribute them to moral laxity; moral laxity could not explain the suddenness of the outbreak.

What had happened was that the very structure of life

Shift of
Horizons

had been changing for a long period without people notic-
ing it; all the external trappings of life were still Catholic
but on a deeper level had moved far down the path of
revolt.

Revolutions are not brought on by propaganda; not
even the magnetic appeal of a gifted personality can cause
them. The milieu as a whole must be ripe for revolution;
the ground must be thoroughly prepared. Revolutions are
not freely caused—they are unleashed.

The extent and the suddenness of the collapse are the
best proof for the extent to which abuses had eaten into
the fiber of the Church.

If we look back on the entire process of shifting values
and withdrawal from the genuine spirit of the Church from
the time of the thirteenth century—in particular the often
radical discontent with the clergy, the confusion in theology, and the weaknesses in popular piety, all occurring at
a time keyed to restlessness and insecurity—then we have
to admit that the radical revolt against the Church, a revolt
which many saw as quite desirable, was quite likely to succeed once it started.

We know that when the Reformation came, its success
was due in no small measure to a number of chance occurrences and elements which were irrelevant as Christian
categories (e.g., the power, willfulness, and even caprice
of spiritual and secular lords and officials); yet this could
only be true if the way for the revolt had been prepared for
centuries by a complex series of events, which unfolded
within the Church. This is the critical point for our discussion.

The most discouraging aspect of the whole situation
is undoubtedly the fact that the revolt which took place
received such impetus from the Church itself. The genuine

Christian conscience, loyal to the Church, was practically forced to protest against many perversions in the Church of the time, precisely in the name of Christianity and the Church. In other words, Catholics must bear a great deal of the responsibility for the revolt.

The extent of the Church's part in causing the revolt against the Church is apparent when we realize that the same perversion of Christian attitudes within the Church also characterized part of the struggle of the Church against the Reformation in its earliest stages. The conclusions to which we are forced by these facts can be summed up in a thesis which is quite painful to us as Catholics. In the struggle of the Church for her very existence against the Reformation, religious forces were employed to a most limited degree and were, in fact, often sacrificed to political concerns, such as the petty politics of individual popes and their families. It is obvious that in this life and death struggle, people had the right to expect just the opposite— a real mobilization of all that was vital in religion.

The proof of our thesis is evident in the actions of Alexander, the papal legate at Worms. In all of the diplomatic correspondence that he sent back to Rome day by day, even in Holy Week, there is no hint of the fact that the proceedings of the Diet were a matter for prayer. In regard to the Catholic theologians who entered the controversy, religious conviction and a feeling for the richness of their resources are almost totally absent from their quite correct and unfortunately pedantic presentations of Catholic doctrine. In this respect they are a poor second to Luther's writings.

Another lamentable fact should be brought out. On three different occasions, the Reformation was saved by a pope—not intentionally of course, but the fact is that these popes were objectively responsible. This is clearest in the case of Leo X. In the year 1518 he had the secret process against Luther opened, and Luther was condemned as a heretic. Then because of the death of Maximilian, the Curia was forced to make a decision on the new emperor. Its choice fell on the Prince who ruled Luther's own territory and immediately the process against Luther was suspended and treated as though it had simply not taken place. Luther was given a reprieve of almost twenty months during which time his new ideas were able to take root.

Condemnation of a man as a heretic is a serious matter. Once the condemnation has taken place, it is a betrayal of the truth to act as though it simply had not happened. We certainly cannot expect that off in Rome, Pope Leo X should have had as full and accurate a knowledge of all the events as could have been had in Germany. Still less could it be known either in Rome or in Germany that the Church was involved in a life and death struggle which would shake the world to its very foundations. It is not fair to anaylze and evaluate the events of a given period exclusively through hindsight; however, this does not detract one iota from the objective failure of the Pope.

Let us sum up the results of our inquiry. Möhler was probably right when he said that everything would have turned out all right if only events had been patiently allowed to take their course. One cannot be a real Catholic without conceding this possibility. Precisely as Catholics, however, we must contradict the principle involved, for it is a fundamental truth of Catholic theology that grace presupposes nature, builds on it, and leaves the natural laws of growth untouched. The natural data involved here were the causes of the Reformation as we have depicted them. As we have seen, the historian would be forced to

judge, after examining them, that the Reformation was
hardly to be avoided, but had, in fact, become a historical
necessity. The split had been coming for a long time and
was very deep by now. From the outside, it still looked as
though the Church held a position of leadership, but in
both public and private life many had come to the point
where they were only a step away from separation from the
Church. The great problem of deciding whether Christian
life was being lived in genuine fashion or only superficially
had reached critical proportions for the Church. Because
the split was so deep, when Luther's act came, it carried all
before it; the depth of this split explains the rapidity of the
collapse throughout Northern Europe.

Despite all of this, as in the case of all events which
have a profound effect on history, the Reformation remains
mysterious. The more we study the sources, the more we
see this. Everything pointed in the direction of a violent
revolt, everything seemed to be waiting for it. But why did
it not come from within, leaving the Church intact? Life
is a mystery that can never be fully resolved, even with the
advantage of hindsight. History in the real sense of the
word, like the critical decisions of human life, crystallizes
in quiet depths closed to the prying eyes of the world. The
great crises that rock humanity are not the results of intellectual dynamism alone and they cannot be understood if
we think that only intellectual factors are involved. They
are vital movements which in many ways are not subject
to interpretation and understanding. When we deal with a
great creative personality, there are many mysterious elements of this type. Reform was just as possible and necessary in 1480 as in 1517, but it came in 1517 when, after
his ideas had been developing in secret for many years,
Luther entered upon the stage of history.

The questions, however, implicit in these last few paragraphs have to be answered. One point in all of our discussions remains untouched; it is not subject to argument and it cannot be passed over in silence. Catholic forces, factors in the Catholic sphere, had their full share in the preparation and the provocation of the Reformation. In other words, the Reformation is a Catholic concern in the sense that Catholics had a large part in bringing it about and were in large measure responsible for it.

Catholics must bear much of the guilt of the Reformation, but this term is to be rightly understood. We are not interested in blaming individuals; the word "guilt" as it is used here does not refer primarily to personal failures whether on the part of the clergy or the laity.

In the period under consideration extraordinarily strong and even conclusive proofs for personal guilt do exist, but ultimately this is the concern of God and the individual conscience. Just as a man is not justified in his actions because he is not conscious of his guilt (1 Cor. 4:4), so we cannot conclude from the visible failures of others to true interior guilt. Above all we are not concerned with the question of whether and to what extent individuals, even many individuals, resisted or did not resist the will of God. We are concerned with the course of historical events, the growth or decay of the whole Church, the increase and decrease of the visible kingdom of God, and the laws that determine these events.

Nowhere are the private and public sides of life so closely intertwined as they are in the Kingdom of God "which is within you" (Luke 17:21). But we cannot draw safe conclusions about the one from events in the other, and it is not the business of the Christian to judge. Therefore, in our discussion, the question of personal and moral guilt is not of decisive importance. The important thing is whether objective failures occurred, whether insufficient action was taken. As we have said before, the message of the kingdom of Christ was not being preached, but a world of difference separates historical causality from the sphere of personal moral guilt. Those persons who are the historical causes of severe deficiencies and critical illnesses in society bear an historical guilt and historical responsibility. We are taking this term in the deep religious sense which it has won in the Communion of Saints and in the Church throughout the centuries. The conclusion we have reached regarding Catholic responsibility and guilt comes to this: The Reformation is a Catholic concern or must become a Catholic concern. For us, as Christians, guilt calls unconditionally for a *mea culpa* as a condition for discharging the task which we have undertaken. If we do not make this confession, human understanding and Christian purification both will elude us.

Pope Adrian VI gave us an example in the confession of guilt we summarized previously. Some Catholics have felt that his confession was not politically shrewd. True enough. Yet we are not in the realm of politics but that of religion, the realm of Christianity, the religion of *metanoia* and the Cross. Ultimately, the true mark of Christianity cannot be political expediency. Christianity grows according to different laws that are not always clear to human reason. But according to these laws of Christian growth, the confession of guilt made by Adrian, who personally lived such a blameless life, was the condition for that renewal within the Church, which, despite all the difficulties, weaknesses and inadequacies, grew, and finally gave us a magnificent century of saints. More of this later.

It will be enough now if we realize that the Reformation

96]   The Reformation:

is a Catholic concern in the sense that Catholics had an important rôle to play in causing it and must share the guilt. We must make the Reformation our concern as Catholics; we must shoulder our guilt. We have seen in our discussion that many of the failures of the pre-Reformation period were directly traceable to the fact that the vital forces of Christianity, the religious factors, were not tapped. But we will not make the same mistake today. If we are to conceive anew the task of the Reformation and discharge this task in the proper way, we will have to mobilize precisely these religious forces. We must seek the truth in love and, above all, introduce prayer into our work. May God who is the master of all history grant us success. I can never tire of repeating that the high-priestly prayer of Our Lord, "that they may all be one," is not something which we say merely out of devotion; it is our duty.

II

Martin Luther:
From Monk to Reformer

In the first chapter we tried to show how it was possible for the Reformation to occur and was practically historical necessity. In this chapter we begin our study of what actually happened, restricting ourselves to the principal causal factor operative in the Reformation: Martin Luther. Again, we are not interested in all the aspects of Luther's life, but specifically in the chain of events that led to his becoming a reformer.

In a sense, our discussion will be a sequel to the treatment of the earlier problem of explaining the possibility of the Reformation, because Luther developed in a Catholic world and his roots were thoroughly Catholic. Insofar as this is true, our task is an examination of our Catholic conscience. It will be immediately apparent, however, that the scope of this chapter will go far beyond this and broaden out into a critique of Luther, involving an examination of the Protestant conscience as well.

Little need be said about the breadth of view that this study demands. We are in search of truth, but, aware of our responsibility, we seek it in charity. Our love of the Catholic Church cannot be permitted to limit our love for our Protestant brethren; rather it should make that love grow. We know that the Reformation has had a profound effect on the destiny of mankind. It will be our aim to achieve anew in our own day what it tried to achieve in the sixteenth century. The approach this demands of us is not too hard for the Christian, for tradition itself supplies us with the necessary philosophical and historical categories. All history is the *opus Dei*; nothing happens apart from the will of the Father who is in heaven. In addition, the Christian has that useful category of the *felix culpa,* the blessed fall, which is illuminating and revealing when we are ultimately forced to reject once and for all the error involved.

Applying this to our theme, we are not going to try Luther for heresy. To be sure, it is a theological and historical fact of the first importance that Luther was condemned as a heretic. Historically and theologically, it would be foolish and harmful to act as though this had not occurred, and we will not lay ourselves open to that charge. Luther, however, has been tried for heresy for too long a period in a thoroughly narrow-minded way. Our concerns are different. We believe that they are not only more timely, but, to put it bluntly, more objectively worthwhile. Our thinking must be governed by charity. We believe that Augustine was right when he said that truly profound knowledge is achieved only in charity. Actually, no trial, even for heresy, should ever be held unless the judgment is to be motivated by charity, and it is an unfortunate fact that frequently in the course of centuries this was not the case. Often enough, this phenomenon can be explained by reason of the particular conditions imposed by place and time, but it does indicate something wrong with the Christian scale of values.

Neither are we interested in the subjective guilt incurred by Luther in the course of his life, particularly because of his attack on the Church and his founding of a new one. This was an important question for Luther alone as he stood before God, and God alone knows the answer. Any answer we might attempt to give would be highly uncertain and quite irrelevant to our purpose. Our question is simply this: In the objective order of things, how did Martin Luther, the monk, become a reformer?

Our task is not simply historical because we want to decide, as objectively as possible, whether the new solutions that Luther proposed were right or wrong. We have discussed this point in our first chapter from the viewpoint of believing Christians, and, in my own case, as a Catholic. We always presuppose that there is such a thing as Christian revelation in the strict sense of the word; that there is such a thing as inviolable dogma, which is far more than an external formulation, but is rather a distant reflection and guarantee of the mystery of our salvation.

To examine events from this point of view is not to forsake the historical and critical method or to impose our own categories on the facts. Actually all we are doing is using Luther's own criteria and judging events as he would have wanted. Luther's only desire was to give the correct interpretation of the *one* corpus of Christian doctrine that bound all Christians. He always wanted his teaching to be measured by the words of Scripture and we should assess Luther and his work by using the same norms that he considered binding. Otherwise, it would be quite unhistorical to try to understand Luther as a reformer by using the subjectivistic categories of liberal Protestantism. The same is, of course, true in regard to our understanding of any outstanding person. This is quite obvious in the case of the great national heroes. We often show the right feeling for this if we restrict our interest to the intellectual efforts of an individual, without concern whether his efforts were crowned with success or not.

Luther's life, his sufferings and achievements, which were a radical departure from the old ways, do not derive their significance from the mysterious factors at the depths of the personality that produced them. This seems strange when we realize the frightful internal struggles experienced by Luther, but we must remember that Luther himself conceived of all of his innovations in terms of the absolutely binding character of revelation. Luther saw that the value of his preaching depended on one thing alone: whether that preaching presented the whole of revelation, no more, no less.

A study of the world-wide repercussions that Luther's doctrine produced in history is not revelant here, for the ultimate Christian norm is truth and dogma, not success. On this point, Catholics and Lutherans are in agreement and differ radically from the modern school, whether the latter be hostile to dogma or simply indifferent to it.

It is quite obvious that we need enough vision to distinguish the genius from the pedant. We cannot apply the norms of ordinary verse to the great literary epics. However, as I mentioned before, where revelation is concerned, even a genius is not a law unto himself. A thoroughly objective study is needed before a judgment can be given; the cursory analysis and type of refutation usually given in the classroom do not suffice. We must be strong enough to search into the depths of a man's personality without fear, though in Luther's case the depths are at times a seething mass of conflicting ideas and emotions which present certain dangers. We need, nevertheless, the courage and the strength to approach at close range.

We have to begin with the fact that Luther was a genius, a man who put his stamp on the period in which he lived, a man endowed with an amazing variety of gifts. To maintain these in equilibrium would be an achievement that demanded a struggle very different from that faced by the ordinary man.

It may be asked whether a gifted genius can be subjected to criticism as ordinary men can or is simply above it. This was the rather foolish objection of the liberals with their "great man myth." Truth is unique, objective; it existed before any man appeared on the scene of history. Luther would be the first to agree with this.

We have to examine the facts with a calm eye, subject them to objective criticism, and force them to yield their real meaning. Our conclusion in the course of the first chapter is quite pertinent here. Not even the very great, even those who have attained the height of fame, can escape being judged by the objective norm of truth. They are capable of error and injustice, and if careful and exact scholarship shows that a genius has gone wrong, the demands made on him or those inspired by him are just as categorical as would be the case if an average man had made the error.

No one who believes in the unity of truth will deny that the history of human thought contains many examples of erroneous developments, and no one can exclude the possibility, *a priori,* that these occurred in the life and work of Martin Luther. We have to keep our minds open or at least learn to do so. In the case of the man who believes in the unity of truth but who is not accustomed to thinking in terms of dogma, he may need to go through quite a period of training. The great events of history demand that we approach them with a certain reverence for their vital reality if we are to learn anything from them. Our approach demands both real commitment and detached objectivity, and with this in mind we turn to Martin Luther.

Two characteristics strike us immediately: Luther was an amazingly rich and complex personality, and an extremely original one. He is a mine of inexhaustible wealth, amazingly productive in his writings and sermons. In a brief time he had a large number of books on the market. Luther is one of those men whose books simply cannot be reduced to a limited outline; any time a section is abstracted and then compared with its original context, it is surprising to see how ineffective the detached section is, how completely out of its own element. Luther is, in the ultimate sense of the word, an individual. It is true that all of his vast work is based on a small number of basic principles to which he recurs again and again. The presence of these fundamental themes in all his work is part of the mystery of Luther and the effectiveness of his work. These motifs are not merely repeated; Luther is always expressing them in new forms and connections. Driven by faith and the needs of preaching he is ceaselessly trying to get to the heart of them. He is always the master of his basic principles, expanding and deepening their field of application.

This is first of all true of Luther's work up to the year 1525. The great struggle that had so essential an influence on his formation and had stamped his character once and for all was aimed at liberating him from an oppressive burden; a specific bond that chained him had to be broken. It is quite understandable that after this goal was reached internally and then externally manifested, Luther's own struggle lost much of its momentum. The result was that some of Luther's characteristics, given above, do not really apply to him after 1525. On the other hand, his marriage and the completion of his significant systematic work *Vom geknechteten Willen* did not make him a lazy man. He never stopped learning and it is noteworthy that even as an old man he was ready to approach the "Our Father" again and seek to penetrate its depths, to "learn" it. This amazing drive was, of course, partially inspired by the necessity of defending his life and work time and time again.

To be sure, the fact that Luther's work was from start to finish too dependent on the man's own peculiar make-up, the uniqueness of his situation and special endowments, causes a great deal of difficulty. Undoubtedly this is unfortunate in the realization of the universal truths, laws, and demands of Christianity which hold for all men at all times. Even after 1525, Luther defended his gains frequently with means that had not been sufficiently checked for their validity. (Note, for example, the sophistry involved in the important question of the private Mass as it appeared in 1533.) But in this period as well as later on, Luther was far from merely repeating himself.

Luther was also a highly original man, but here we must distinguish between the theologian and the reformer. The practical demands of Luther the reformer reflect not only the needs of the sixteenth century; he simply takes many of them directly from the writings of the earlier reformers. His true originality was as a theologian.

It is true that Luther was also dependent on the theology of his own day, as he learned it from his professors—in other words, on a form of Ockhamist theology. This is so true that, unless the intellectual seed had been planted in his course of theology, it can be shown that Luther would never have become a reformer. This can be proved by a simple experiment. Take a good, modern, preferably Protestant study of Luther's development and subtract the ideas which are Ockhamist in origin. Immediately all the elements which caused the friction, sparked the struggle, and ultimately led to the open break, vanish. The "reformation" elements in Luther are so closely connected with the traditional theses of Ockhamist theology that without the latter it is simply impossible to explain Luther's revolt rationally.

And yet it is true that Luther was essentially independent of his Ockhamist background and that the latter had no influence on Luther's most distinctive characteristics. The real sources of Luther's development are all within him, in the dynamic factors at the very core of his personality. His struggle was a lonely one, inaccessible to others, and it is impossible to follow the course of his development step by step. In spite of Luther's dependence on the tradition in which he was educated, it is true in a deeper sense that absolutely no one had a part in Luther's formation.

Moreover, from his earliest days, he manifests great independence of the authorities of tradition to a dangerous degree—he rejects Aristotle, as he had been taught by his Ockhamist teachers, but also extends this attitude to Thomas Aquinas and even Augustine. One can easily see what an advantage this independence in regard to the tradition was for the professor who was later to organize the new University of Wittenberg. He was quite unrestricted and free to indulge his penchant for innovation. However, there is an obvious danger here in the intellectual as well as the religious sphere that became acute in the case of a man like Luther, with his absolutely unique character, his lack of balance, and his tendency to see only one side of any question all of which made calm and balanced judgment so difficult. This attitude was dangerous in the intellectual sphere because tradition is one of the indispensable factors in intellectual life, which can exist only as a continuum. No one can attain truth by working alone; no one can reject the intellectual achievements of past generations without paying a penalty—too many truly valuable acquisitions will be lost.

This is especially true in the case of Christianity, where it is of prime importance to preserve intact the whole deposit of faith. This cannot be done if an individual breaks abruptly with the past and tries to negate a thousand years of tradition. When Luther did this, he faced the immediate danger of being quite revolutionary and of failing to preserve intact the inviolable, objective data of revelation. He offered not acceptable renovation, but inacceptable innovation.

It is difficult to give an adequate picture of Luther. Despite all the information we have from himself and others, despite all that we know about his life and work—information so detailed that we can follow the events of his life almost to the day and the hour—and despite the fact that for four hundred years, generations of scholars of all persuasions have written an immense (and often confusing) number of volumes on Luther, scholars still are unable to agree on a judgment of Luther and his work. Interpretations differ radically; not only Protestants and Catholics differ in their judgment, but within the Protestant camp there is an amazing variety of opinion. The different interpretations of Luther that have appeared over the last centuries serve only to warn us of the shortsightedness and prejudice of a number of "scholars."

Even today, within Protestant scholarly circles, there are a number of sharply opposing schools of thought, not only on unessential points, but on the essential doctrines of Luther's work. Are we to see in this merely an expression of the inexhaustible richness of Luther's activity, or are we to attribute it to instability in Luther's own thought?

It would seem easy to speak to Protestants on the subject of Luther, but actually it is quite difficult. The main reason is a great temptation to paint as bright a picture as possible and to see only the positive elements in his character. It is even more difficult to do justice to Luther when speaking to a Catholic audience because they tend to think of Luther only as the heretic, the man who attacked their Church and hurt it as no other man before or since. Both these difficulties can be avoided only by giving a picture of the whole Luther, that is, not trying to include every single detail, but noting everything essential in his character. It is easy to see Luther only as a hero, a man who made great positive contributions to his age; it is also easy to see only his mistakes and weaknesses and to condemn him for them. There is plenty of material available for either approach and both have been far too common, but for us neither will do.

We seek to understand the contradictory features in Luther's character. Avoiding either extreme, we attempt to see the good with the bad, praising the real contributions he made and, where necessary, finding fault with him for the harm he did. We will aim not at a tiresome tabulation of pros and cons, but at a unified, composite view, keeping both elements in mind at the same time.

This is the only way in which Protestants and Catholics can hope to come to a common scholarly ground on the subject of Luther. Our procedure will be different from that used heretofore; we cannot decide *a priori* what Luther was and then proceed to interpret him and his work from this highly subjective concept. Rather we have to proceed inductively, almost statistically, examining what Luther had to say on all of the main points of doctrine. Then we will be able to tell to what extent the main lines of Luther's doctrine are firmly drawn and to what extent there was vacillation in his own mind. Was Luther an exact thinker, or does his thought and expression wander quite freely within a vaguely defined area?

Many problems make it difficult to give an adequate picture of Luther. One is that Luther's own statements on the same matters show much variation at different times. Harnack, for example, recognized that at times they approached the point of absolute contradiction. Other factors are Luther's tendency to exaggerate, his intemperate style of expression, and the polemic concern that permeated all his work.

Essentially, however, the difficulty stems from the peculiarities of Luther's own mental make-up, which can be briefly formulated in the following way: Luther's inspiration was not primarily intellectual, nor was his work careful and systematic; emotion had a dominant rôle in his work. This is not to underestimate the intellectual value of Luther's work; its scope was wide and penetrating, but the distinctive note responsible for the originality in Luther's message is personal involvement and commitment.

His capacity for personal involvement in a situation was joined with great strength of will. He is relentless in hammering out solutions to the problems that faced him, and so deeply involved in the inner struggle that at times he has eyes for nothing but the pressing and immediate problems of the day, even of the moment. The solution to *this* difficulty, here and now, alone can give him inner peace. This most unique characteristic shows how far Luther was from the spirit of calm and objective reflection that makes a synthesis possible. His dialectic was essentially exclusive.

In recent years, Protestant scholarship has tried to de-emphasize the personal and emotional factors in Luther's work, but in my opinion, they have gone too far in confusing the more objective spirit of Luther's earlier lectures with the factors that influenced his development as a theologian. His development was quite unlike that common in scholastic circles; thus it would be most imprudent to compare his interpretations with theirs, though it is true that at the time of his first lectures on the Psalms he was far from the radical spirit he manifested in his theses on indulgences. This tendency to de-emphasize the emotional elements in Luther's makeup cannot be reconciled either with Luther's war on monasticism, or with his observations on his own development, or with the great degree of personal commitment manifest in all his work.

Finally, the thesis that Luther's theological development was conditioned by purely objective factors would put a severe strain on his veracity. Today both Protestant and Catholic scholarship is in agreement on the fact that in Luther's work there are grave misconceptions and objectively massive false assertions. To call these objectively false assertions lies seems to me to be far too superficial a judgment, precisely because Luther's development is essentially dependent on a mysterious inner world of personal involvement and emotional reaction. If this is denied, then I fail to see how Luther can escape the charge of consciously perverting the truth. It is nevertheless true that in later years emotion played a less significant rôle in Luther's life than it did in the early revolt.

Another fact worthy of note is that Luther was endowed with unusual gifts of expression which he could place at the disposal of his genius. He was able to give perfectly apt expression to the intertwined and violent forces at the depths of his personality. The man who reads Luther's writings is present on most intimate terms to his inner experience. Luther's words overwhelm and almost overpower the reader. Packed with meaning, coming directly to the point, filled with suggestive images, rhythmically phrased, with real ear-appeal, his writing employs all the variations appropriate to the profound appeals he is making.

Of course not all that Luther wrote is worthy of this high praise. His literary work was so wide in scope and frequently composed in haste under unfavorable conditions that the same high level could not always be maintained. Some of his material is boring; sometimes he repeats himself endlessly, and at times his adaptation of words and concepts from scholastic Latin put a severe strain on the German idiom. Even in the splendid translation of the Bible on which he expended so much care and diligence, there are some sections that are quite clumsy, for Luther was no litterateur. He had some of the literary tendencies of the humanist; he had a feeling for sound and rhythm; his verse (not including, of course, his disgraceful ditties that went with Cranach's mocking cartoons of the popes) and much of his prose prove this, but the religious and pastoral content of his message so dominated his interest that he did not have much time for polishing up the expression. The latter took care of itself. It was simply there, and in the main it is attractive, quite striking, and flexible.

Taking both of these elements together, the intensely personal view Luther took of everything and the peculiar gifts of expression that were his, it is clear that he would have a tendency to use superlatives and exclusive formulations. He is not a man to worry about the exact shades of meaning or carefully weighed statements. In former days, Catholic polemic literature used to refer to Luther as the *Doctor Hyperbolicus,* and not without reason. The term noted a decisive point, even though it did not succeed in understanding and assessing it correctly.

The impressiveness of Luther's expression was due in large measure to the fact that almost every word was the echo of one or other of the battles he fought up to the day of his death. His statements reflect his inner life and struggles; he paid dearly for all his convictions, and they were most effective for that reason.

We mentioned hitherto vacillations in Luther's doctrine; these depend, in the main, on Luther's own peculiar mentality but especially on the predominance of emotional factors. These derive their vitality from a paradoxical structure, indicating thus the basic structure of Luther's theology, particularly his theology of the Cross. For him, contradiction is an indication of divine knowledge and power; paradox was his chosen form of creative expression. For Luther paradox had many advantages: it indicated the unintelligible and inconceivable aspects of the Christian mysteries, while penetrating deeply into their content. It is, after all, a paradox that Jesus Christ, the Son of God become man, when He was dying on the cross as an outcast and a criminal, cried out: "My God, My God, Why has Thou forsaken Me?"

Luther's character manifested an unusually excessive introversion. He was absolutely convinced that he alone was right, that he was his own pope, speaking *ex cathedra*. He had a reckless kind of boldness that knew no bounds. The demagogic force that moved him would at times indulge in the wildest arguments, holding on to its own opinion through thick and thin. Consequently, in thinking and speaking paradoxically, Luther was often in danger of contradicting himself by one and the same formula, which he actually did on a number of different matters. This tendency of Luther, together with the impetuous way his judgments and demands were put, constitutes one of the greatest stumbling blocks in our dialog concerning the Reformation, for even the Protestants of today are heirs of this type of theological thought. The influence of Luther's own tremendous vitality has prevailed here, and in so doing has shown its most dangerous side.

The later reflections on his development that Luther himself has left us are an important and, in many respects, definitive source for our knowledge of him. Many of the things he tells us simply contradict the objective facts of his development of which we are certain, whether we use certain earlier statements of the reformer himself as a guide, or reconstruct the actual situation from other sources. Are we to call Luther a liar because of these contradictions? By no means! The category of "liar" is far too superficial— it does not reach to the real depths of his personality. A number of things can be explained simply by the inevitable short-sightedness that afflicts anyone who tries to reconstruct events from his early life. The very fact that he was utterly absorbed in his interior life during the period of his development will account for a certain lack of clarity. In addition, as he looked back on his life in the monastery, his life as a Catholic, he had an unavoidable temptation to paint as black a picture as possible and to conceive a real hatred against this period in which, as we will see, he suffered so much. Above all, we have to remember that Luther's development was unlike anything any of us have experienced; with him it was practically a substantial change, involving the interplay of deep and violent forces in a gifted personality. It was hardly possible that in later years, after the long process of development was over and his thought had crystallized once and for all, he would be able to recognize and describe for us just what his exact situation had been at any given moment.

Now that we have sketched the general picture, we will try to answer the question of how the Catholic monk, Martin Luther, became a heretic and a reformer.

The first time we have a chance to know much about Luther is at his entrance into religion; to be sure we have one or two details about his childhood and youth, but these are of minor importance. Our picture of Luther begins to fill out when he entered the monastery at Erfurt and embraced the religious life. This is extremely significant, for whatever else Luther was or became, he remained first and last a religious man. The absolute reality of God (not just a concept of God) occupied a central place in his consciousness. Throughout the whole span of his life he had little difficulty in approaching God and raising his heart to Him in prayer.

Luther was fundamentally a religious man; some have acted as though this is rather insignificant, but in my opinion it is a real honor to be characterized as such, particularly if one has as clearcut a title to it as does Luther.

We have relatively few accounts of Luther's life in the monastery, and yet it was for him a period of great importance, a time when he became involved in the difficulties to which he was to apply so radical a solution. During that period he underwent profound development. Luther's conscience was alone before God. That was the distinctive aspect of his life in the monastery, and the development he underwent was gradual although, at times, spasmodic. Individual tendencies to radical solutions appear from time to time, and together with the gradual shifting of values which took place, they produced the outlook of a full-fledged reformer. In his later reflections, Luther simplified this picture in dramatic fashion and compressed the events. He himself was no longer able to reconstruct the events in ex-

act detail, and today we are even less able to do so. Many
elements were indirectly and unconsciously rejected and
vanished, while on the other hand, many elements were
preserved that in the passion of the moment seemed to be
rejected. Few external factors had much influence on
Luther's development; the distinctively original elements in
Luther developed from within, from the depths of his
personality.

At that period, Luther's whole interior life was dominated by the tension between his obligations and his power
to discharge them. Because of his background of popular
Catholic teaching, a certain scrupulosity of disposition and
Ockhamist theology, he was obsessed with the notion of
becoming reconciled to God through his own powers, of
being obliged to attain sanctity by his own actions; in this
all-important matter, he experienced failure again and
again.

This tension and Luther's own attitude were responsible
for the great struggles of soul which led to the outbreak of
the Reformation. They depend essentially first on Luther's
life in the monastery and his struggle for perfection in the
framework of a particular religious and ascetical system
and secondly, on the theology of the Bible, particularly of
the New Testament.

The first definite conclusion from what we know about
these struggles is that Luther took them very seriously. A
favorable indication of this is that Luther did not enter a
lax monastery: he entered a strict monastery of the Hermits
of St. Augustine where the rule was observed with pristine
vigor. What we know of Luther's life in the monastery in
the period when his doctrine was still fundamentally Catholic confirms this.

Above all, in the revolutionary development that followed, we are dealing with an unintentional process of change, with an unintended movement away from the Church. This slow and indeliberate process of growth, accompanied by profound struggles of conscience, caused his convictions to sink deep and ineradicable roots.

We have to be quite clear about this unintentional process of development which was so dependent on his inner struggles and carried on almost in isolation. Then we can understand what a shock it must have been for Luther when in the dispute over indulgences he came up against the popular Catholic mind, or when in his dispute with Cardinal Cajetan and Eck he came into conflict with a type of theology utterly foreign to his own highly personal experience and views.

In the monastery, Luther's main source of spiritual nourishment was the Bible. It was not as though he flouted the will of superiors in reading the Bible as some formerly thought. Rather it was the monastic rule itself which prescribed the reading of the Bible and which, in the practical order, provided him with the whole Bible, bound in red leather, for reading and study. It was then that something quite unusual happened: Luther applied himself with unusual vigor to the Book of Books, and the Bible answered his needs to such an extent that there resulted that extraordinary inner relationship between Luther and the Bible which he later compared correctly to a marriage. In practically no time Luther knew whole sections of the Bible by heart. He made them his own to such an extent and they had such an essential rôle in his development that in later years the words of the text were always at his disposal in his letters, lectures, and probably in hearing confessions as well as when he was busy about pastoral work.

Martin Luther: From Monk to Reformer   [117

The Bible was the source of Luther's inspirations; from it he drew a wealth of religious content for himself and others.

But Luther's development, nourished by the Bible, resulted in his leaving the Church. How was that possible? Did Luther see the fundamental facts about the Church which his monastic training and theology offered in the right light and did he make the right use of them? Or was he one-sided in his outlook? Furthermore, did his theology really give Brother Martin a thoroughly Catholic foundation? This is the point we wish to investigate.

Just as today, in Luther's time a man would be received into a religious house as a novice and would pronounce vows according to a determined rite with certain customary prayers. In his later years, Luther never tired of pointing out that in the Catholic Church there was nothing but hypocrisy and that Catholics taught that grace and salvation could be earned through a man's own works. With untiring emphasis and with a severity that at times smacked of hatred, Luther affirmed this of religious life.

Now we know the prayers that were spoken over Brother Martin as he received his cassock and pronounced his vows. They contain a few references to merit, in no way subject to overemphasis or isolation, but remain subordinate to the main content of these prayers—that grace is everything, that man can do nothing on his own, and again that God, who had begun the good work in Brother Martin, would bring it to a successful conclusion. Luther's entry into religious life in the monastery was not done in a framework of hypocritical ceremonies; these ceremonies were permeated by the doctrine of grace.

But Luther had not made this doctrine his own, though it was quite obviously present in those prayers. It seems that he was simply blind to it. It would seem that from other sources he had somehow gotten the erroneous idea that man had to rely on his own powers to effect a reconciliation with God. This notion so dominated all his thinking that he was unable to break out of the closed circle.

Luther was soon ordained (1506). For every priest, the experience of celebrating his First Mass is of the greatest importance. For a man like Luther, who was so powerfully governed by the emotional level of experience, it was of even greater importance. He has left us a number of accounts of his First Mass. If we take the essential elements of these, we find that according to Luther he was so profoundly moved that he would have been swept from the altar if the assistant priest had not held him back. It may be questioned whether he was really tempted to rush from the altar. Perhaps in later years he was yielding to the tendency to speak in superlatives, but there is no doubt that he was profoundly moved. Luther also tells us why: he was deeply impressed by the nearness of the awesome majesty of God, who is addressed in the Canon as the living and true God.

Luther's experience shows us first of all that he was a religious man, forced to his knees as it were by the tremendous reality of God. We see in his experience something which cannot without some restrictions be called healthy. Does this entitle us to speak of mental illness in his case? We see that he was often profoundly moved, subject to strong depressions, restless at intervals, and, later in life, subject to violent changes of temper. All of this is quite apparent and shows that Luther had a tempestuous character, and that in his soul raged forces that were beyond his power to control. It tells us, too, that we are dealing with a soul obsessed with anxiety in the face of sin and the divine judgment and caught in the net of scrupulosity. But scrupulosity is a weakness proper to a tender conscience; thus there is no reason to speak of mental illness in the proper sense of the word, at least at the time of his First Mass. This possibility is further excluded when we realize the tremendous amount and the fine quality of the works that Luther produced unceasingly. (Whether one could speak of a psychosis in Luther's case in the more restricted medical sense of the word is a matter for psychiatrists and does not concern us here.) At any rate we should be quite clear about the meaning of "mentally ill." It seems that the rather loosely used schema "manic depressive" (when it is not used in the sense of insanity) can be quite easily verified in the average mentally healthy individual if that individual is unusually sensitive. It is quite easy to say what Luther was not: he was not balanced, moderate or prudent, not restrained; one might say that he was quite uninhibited, that in a typically Germanic way he escapes classification and categorization. His lack of restraint is shown by all sorts of exaggerations; they indicate a violent impulsiveness which extends even to the falsification of objective facts in such impossible forms that the reader is utterly amazed. What Christian conscience will, for example, be able to accept his statement that he preferred Christ to all the devils, because he stood in such deadly terror of Him?

Whether the violent depressions of the year 1527/8 are correctly described by the Danish psychiatrist Paul Reiter as mental illness in the strict sense, is a matter for doctors to decide. But the entire mental structure and the intellectual and spiritual work Luther turned out (as Reiter himself admits), show that mental illness is by no means a sufficient explanation. At any rate it is impossible to declare simply that Luther was mentally ill. If one were so inclined, a whole book could be filled with individual examples which point in the direction of mental illness, but if we are going to keep a just proportion, we would have to match this with ten or more volumes which would positively prove Luther's mental, spiritual, and religious health.

The one conclusion we can come to now from Luther's experience at his First Mass is that he was entirely preoccupied with the anxiety that he felt as, with all his sins, he stood alone before the sovereign majesty of God. It is true that in the Canon, the living and true God is directly addressed, and that the Canon is preceded by the solemn, threefold *Sanctus* addressed to the divine majesty, but that is not the whole story.

The Preface has nothing of the awesome and exalted tone of the *Sanctus;* rather this prayer is a great lifting of the mind and heart, a great surge of adoration and praise which embraces heaven and earth and joins the voices of men to the song of the angels, but Luther was unaware of all this.

Furthermore, the Canon itself begins with the wonderful and consoling words: *"Te igitur, clementissime Pater, per Jesum Christum, Filium Tuum, Dominum Nostrum, supplices rogamus."* That is: "We humbly call upon Thee, most merciful Father, through Jesus Christ, Thy Son, our Lord." God is not addressed as the Judge who threatens to punish all the defects, but as a kind and loving Father. And the sinner approaches the Father not on his own, but through our Saviour, the Mediator, Jesus Christ. This is precisely the formula which Luther will later say contains all of the Christian message, but for some reason Luther did not see it then. He undoubtedly knew these words by heart as he did the rest of the Canon, but did not realize them. He was so deeply involved in those ideas which he had

from his early days, the preaching he had heard, the Ockhamist theology he had learned, and above all his own
peculiar disposition and correspondingly unique experiences, that he was simply blind to the solution for which he
was striving so violently and which was given to him here,
word by word.

This was so characteristic of Luther. He could not
accept anyone else's solution. He was so individualistic and
in a sense so narrow that only solutions of his own appeared valid. Luther was capable of assimilating only those
things which were adapted to the peculiarities of his personality. He was an individual in the strictest sense of the
word and this influenced his every act; it was the source of
both his greatness and his limitations.

Here again we see a fact of primary importance: Luther
never really understood the Missal as a compendium of
the theology of grace and the sacraments. Some have objected to the emphasis I place on Luther's experience at his
First Mass or feel that I make too much depend on this
thesis. Luther did finish that Mass and later, at breakfast,
he had been able to talk in calm and collected fashion with
his father; for years afterwards he continued to celebrate
Mass.

The important thing to note, however, is that no one
ever asserted that Luther continued in his disturbed state
for a long time. (If this had happened, beyond doubt he
would have been mentally ill.) But note this: Luther's experience at the time of his First Mass was no isolated or
independent event: it is an instance of the disposition which
was central to Luther's character and caused him so much
trouble. On the one hand he was an introvert, and on the
other, he had a one-sided concept of the severity of an
avenging God who demanded good works of His creature.

If the experience at the time of the First Mass were unique, the objection would be valid; however, the various observations we have made on Luther's life as a young monk agree in the points mentioned, and reinforce one another. Therefore, there is no question of trying to draw too many conclusions just from the First Mass.

In Luther's experience at the time of his First Mass, the same struggles of conscience appear which beset him in the monastery. Naturally, Luther's later assertions about the unceasing tension he was under are not to be taken too seriously. We know that on occasion he himself described his early life in religion as a calm and peaceful one. But his struggles of conscience were extremely severe. With unending perseverance he tried to get to the bottom of his problems and find a way out. In so doing, he was relentless in the war he waged on himself. We can accuse him of a good deal of imprudence, but we cannot say that he did not take his problems seriously enough. He brought them into the presence of God as he struggled with all his might to reach the complete solution.

Anxiety weighed him down—anxiety at the burden of sin which he saw in himself and which endangered his immortal soul, and made him feel the pains of the damned. (Even if Luther's description of this experience is expressed in terms taken from Tauler and has a rather elaborate literary coloring, still no one can deny that it was part of Luther's objective experience and a burden that weighed terribly on him.)

From the psychological point of view, we have before us a man who was extremely troubled by a serious type of scrupulosity. He had developed a real talent for disputing with himself, bringing forward arguments and counter-arguments, and by so doing, tortured himself by running around in circles.

But the religious aspect is more important. Luther experienced his anxiety so terribly, largely because at one and the same time he longed so profoundly for a kind and loving God. To be free from sin and to reach this kind and loving God was Luther's problem and all his powers were directed to this end.

Luther tried to surmount his difficulties with all the means the Church offered: prayer, asceticism, confession, talks with his spiritual director. Again we must take express note of the fact that if asceticism had its place among these means, we must not see it in the light of the exaggerated picture Luther drew later on in his life. His physical health was never really in danger because of cold or hunger.

The principal means he used was confession and he availed himself of it continually. He had a deep inner affinity for this sacrament. Even in his later days, he told us that he would have despaired without it and that he practiced it up to the end of his life, although he no longer held to the dogma of the Church on the sacrament. But even Confession did not help him in his sufferings; he felt the same tendency toward sin after confession as before, and his sufferings continued. He did not feel that his sins had been forgiven. Without rest or peace, he oscillated between the attempt to break through the bonds that held him and the tendency to fall back into the despairing state of anxiety and sin.

At this time Luther was fortunate in coming in contact with the right men—a piece of good fortune which did not repeat itself at least when he came out in the open as a reformer. At that time, Luther brought all his problems to his Rector, Staupitz. He told him of his sufferings and of the tortures God was inflicting on him. Staupitz had a high opinion of Luther and did a great deal for him; he understood the confused impulsiveness of Luther's character and he showed him that divine grace was the solution, telling him: "You're wrong. God isn't torturing you. You are torturing yourself. Turn your eyes to Jesus Christ on the cross. In His wounds is the source of your salvation." Here again we find the exact formula which Luther was searching for and which he will later say contains all of Christianity. It was being offered to him but in vain. Aside from slight passing improvement, Luther's difficulties remained. It was another case of Luther's inability to be influenced externally; his own emotional experience was the only thing that influenced him.

Again and again we see the same picture: Luther stands alone; he is the lone warrior. He made everything his own. He was never able calmly and patiently to listen in the real sense of the word, in which the heart and soul are receptive to a message and ready to receive it in its fullness. He is a stranger to the attitude which would patiently permit even mysterious and disturbing influences to work on him without reacting at the inopportune moment.

Luther had no understanding for synthesis, the mutual interaction of more than one element, and thus he could not achieve a synthesis for himself. Forcefully and even violently he strove to simplify everything, to see it only in one light, in a one-sided way. It was obvious that for him the objective multiplicity of the real world would be given too little attention and the personal element would receive too much. All our investigations so far converge on one point: Luther is in the fullest sense of the word an individual.

What was the result of all these struggles? His feelings of sinfulness remained and grew worse every day. There was a great danger that a spasmodic outbreak would occur and that he would react in his violent way. Merely to say that indicates how unfavorable the situation was for the realization of the total content of revelation; how dangerous the situation was if one recalls that Luther had the duty of preserving tradition.

We will now examine the theological elements operative in the struggle which so tortured Luther's soul; these elements, of course, had definite Ockhamist and Nominalist tendencies. Luther was not trained as a radical Ockhamist, but in the different forms of a relatively orthodox Ockhamism of the fifteenth century, the dangers, insufficiencies, and blind alleys, which we have pointed out previously, were present.

Ockhamism is in itself a one-sided development which destroyed the harmony of being by isolating the elements of a systematic philosophy. It is not hard to imagine the explosive force of this theology as applied to the *complexio oppositorum* which Catholicism represented when joined with Luther's dangerous individualism and with his tendency to exaggerate. In no time at all, this system was utterly unable to help him find a kind and loving God. If driven to its logical conclusions, it would eventually bring him either to resignation or toward a rejection of previously held dogmas of the faith. But Luther was not resigned; because of his strength of will, he broke out of the system and in so doing rejected some of the tenets of Ockhamism while retaining many others. In so doing he did not imitate the fortunately illogical position of many Ockhamists of his own day who remained Catholic.

Naturally enough, an arbitrary God, or at least a God

who threatened judgment, could not be satisfied by a mere man using his own unaided powers. Here was a difficult problem and one which became insoluble in the unusually dangerous spiritual state in which Luther again and again had eyes for nothing but his own weakness. It was this state of soul and this type of theology which forced Luther to the point of an open break with the Church. Therefore it is extremely important that we should know the extent to which Luther's point of departure was Catholic.

Luther himself thought that his point of departure was Catholic and that in leaving it behind he was abandoning Catholic doctrine. He was wrong. In starting the Reformation Luther was struggling against a Catholicism that was no longer Catholic in the full sense of the word. In this regard it is essential to remember what we saw in the first three chapters about the lack of theological clarity at the end of the fifteenth century and the rôle played by Ockhamist theology. This will shed some interesting light on the problem of the causes of the Reformation: Luther became a reformer because of the theological confusion of his day.

For one thing, Luther did not have a truly Catholic understanding of sin and its forgiveness. From the theology of his day he had imbibed the notion that sinful tendencies were already sins. Then he demands that at every confession and absolution he be able to feel, here and now, that the burden of sin has been removed. Later in life, in an Ash Wednesday sermon of 1529, he formulated the distinction quite exactly, the distinction between faith and feeling. Confession and absolution are strictly in the sphere of faith. When with true contrition, I confess my sins to an ordained priest of the Church and he absolves me, I must accept by faith the fact that my sins are forgiven. We are most

fortunate if our faith takes the concrete form of allowing
us to feel that our sins have been forgiven, but this is not
essential.

A third consideration shows how wanting was the Catholicism against which Luther rebelled. The Church was
not a vital element in Luther's thought (and this was true
of much of the theology of the day). Luther was essentially
a lone worker, even in the cloister.

Thus, our conclusion is this: Luther rebelled against a
Catholicism that was no longer fully Catholic. We can sum
up everything that we have said about Luther by saying
that he was not attentive to the voice of the Church. We
may now ask a further question: Was Luther attentive to
the voice of the Bible?

Luther's theological and religious development is bound
most closely to the word of God found in the New Testament. For him, the word of God became the only norm.
From it he drew all his justification for denying that the
pope and the Roman Church deserved the name of Christian. It may also be asked if Luther was justified in claiming the whole New Testament for himself in this way? Was
Luther thoroughly attentive to the word of God? When I
ask the question, Protestants are usually quite shocked. For
them it is hard to believe that anyone could ask this about
Luther seriously. Isn't it clear and obvious that Luther always wanted himself and his work judged by the criterion
of Scripture, that he always measured himself by this norm
and wanted his doctrine to be so measured?

There is no doubt that Luther wanted to be attentive to
the divine word and nothing more, ready at all times to
submit himself to the judgment of Scripture. Here we are
not concerned with intentions but with facts. What does it
mean to be fully attentive to the word of Scripture? It is

not easy to say, but our discussion will show again and again how important a clear understanding is on this point.

Revelation has been given us by God neither in a single phrase nor in a single book, nor through the tongue or pen of a single inspired writer. We are rather faced with the decisively important fact that the one Gospel of Jesus Christ —to restrict ourselves to the New Testament—was written by different authors, whose intellectual endowments and spiritual gifts differed, sometimes radically. The authors were interested in different aspects of one and the same Gospel, due to their different dispositions and educations. They preached and interpreted the message of Christ in situations whose pastoral demands were quite different. The difference in religious, pastoral and spiritual points of view we find in Matthew, Mark and Luke on the one hand and John on the other, or again in Paul. Think too of the difference between the Gospels and private revelation—all this is obvious and needs no proof. This multiple character of Our Lord's one Gospel has a good effect in that there is no problem concerning religion or the interior life on which Holy Scripture does not have something profound to say.

What are the demands imposed by this many-sided character of the Bible? We are not going to assert that everything in Holy Scripture is of equal value. Christians are again and again brought face to face with the vital problem of finding out what the essence of Revelation is. But this essence, or the formula which expresses this essence, must be broad enough to include everything significant in the Bible. Nothing essential can be left out.

This could be done without danger or difficulty if there were a single set of core-ideas behind the theology of the Bible, but unfortunately that is not the case. Some have tried to do it with Paul's doctrine, but which Paul will we use? The Paul of the Areopagus, the Paul of the Epistle to the Romans? What is the basic theological point of the Epistle to the Romans?

In what sense can we cay that Luther was attentive to the spirit of the Bible? We have already seen how unfavorable Luther's whole mental and spiritual outlook was to accept theological knowledge from outside sources without warping it in the process, changing its key and reducing its content by limiting its scope to his personal experience, even when this knowledge lay along the course of development of his own thought and corresponded well to the very end for which he was striving. Remember how the reality of grace as it appeared in the various monastic prayers completely escaped Luther and that he never really achieved a personal appropriation of the great prayers of the Missal.

We find the same deficiency in Luther in regard to the New Testament during the period of the important developments of his life in the monastery. Above all, Luther, as is abundantly clear by now, did not see the Gospel as the good news of the fact that God is our Father. This was evident from the experience he had at the time of his First Mass. All of his struggles in religious life came from the same source.

There are other indications. In the first place, Luther's erroneous assertions in regard to Romans 1:17. In a well-known later reflection on his early development which Luther has left us in the Preface to the first volume of his collected Latin works published in 1545, in a significant paragraph, he tells us among other things of his definitive decisions that resulted in the Reformation: he found the text of Romans 1:17 a stumbling block and even a scandal, because there it said that divine justice was revealed in the Gospel. "As though it were not enough," he said to himself, "that God had already burdened us with the Ten Commandments; now His justice is to be preached to us even in the Gospel!" For, as Luther says, he had been taught according to the teaching of all medieval doctors that we should always conceive of divine justice as punitive action by which God punishes our sins. He tells us that with a disturbed conscience he came up against this text again and again and murmured blasphemously against God Himself. His attention was finally directed to the context where it is said that the just man lives from faith. Then he realized that here there was no question of punitive justice but of salvific justice, by which God saves us. He tells us that this was a tremendous discovery for him. All of Holy Scripture took on a new light and he felt as though he had emerged into a paradise of freedom. He immediately began to compare other parts of Scripture which he had memorized. He tells us that this confirmed him in his opinion as did the reading of Augustine. Thus he managed to rid himself of his feelings of guilt and of all his interior struggles and threw them off, as he says, on all the Doctors of the Middle Ages.

What about this assertion? The Dominican, Father Denifle, though his understanding of Luther was deficient in some important respects, did have an excellent grasp of many fields connected with medieval theology and was interested in this question. He published his conclusions in a scholarly volume in 1903. He realized that the writers who would have exercised great influence in explaining a text of the Bible were the medieval exegetes. Therefore he examined the writings of about fifty of these who worked on the Epistle to the Romans. He showed that, with perhaps

one exception, the *justitia Dei* of Romans 1:17 was understood as salvific justice, or at least that this interpretation
was beyond a doubt the primary one. Here again Luther
was not able to accept the correct interpretation offered
him by the tradition. He had to come to these conclusions
anew for himself after a period of intense and violent
struggle.

Recently, in addition to other objections already made
by K. Holl, my Protestant colleague Bornkamm of Leipzig
has tried to attack Denifle's proof and my appeal to it. In
his opinion it is not a question of medieval exegesis but of
medieval systematic theology, and he asserts that the latter
teaches without exception that *justitia Dei* of Romans 1:17
was concerned with divine punitive justice.

His proof is not conclusive. In the first place Luther
says that he had been taught by all the Doctors that this
locus was to be understood in the sense of punitive justice.
Even if Bornkamm were right, Luther's assertions would
not be justified and we would be faced at the least with another of Luther's frequent exaggerations. In the second
place, Luther failed to examine the various possibilities in
the tradition with the care that was necessary and in his
case probably obligatory. But Bornkamm is wrong even if
we limit our attention to systematic theology as represented
by Thomas Aquinas. Luther speaks expressly of the *justitia
Dei* as the divine punitive justice but this is an impossible
interpretation of St. Thomas, at least if the claim is made
to give the essentials of his thought, as it is. In St. Thomas,
God's remunerative justice is shown to be permeated with
divine love and mercy and finds its perfection in this fact.
In other words, Thomas emphasized the very reality that
Luther was looking for—a kind and loving God. Only
among Luther's contemporaries was the notion of punitive

justice exaggerated; in other words, here again, our thesis looks good. Luther was a victim of a theology which was no longer fully Catholic.

He was also a victim of his subjective tendency to see only one side of the question; practically he could see God only as a judge, and therefore as a source of punishment and anxiety. He could not free himself from this idea, and any number of proofs could be adduced either from the early or later periods. Time and time again, in later life he repeated the objection that in the Roman Church no one entrusted himself to Christ and had confidence in Him as a Savior. He was rather feared as a strict judge. It is hard to understand how strong a hold this error had on him—a result of his extreme awareness of his own sinfulness, combined with contemporary, popular, Catholic theological thinking and semi-Catholic Ockhamism; however, it is a fact.

This is important for our understanding of the difficulty Luther found in Romans 1:17. In this place, Luther was dealing by no means with an isolated concept of divine justice but with the whole content of verse 17, with the meaning of *divine justice* as used here, and with the question of the content of the whole Gospel. For this reason it is highly significant that Luther interpreted the word as punitive justice. For we all know how much Luther read in Scripture during those years; how he read it as a whole in terms of a particular context and sought understanding in individual cases from Scripture as a whole. Now it is immediately apparent that the context of Romans 1:17 has nothing to do with punishment. On the contrary, from verse 15 where the word *Gospel* appears, the very opposite of punishment is mentioned. "I am ready to preach Gospel to you who are at Rome. For I am not ashamed of the Gospel for it is the

power of God unto salvation to everyone who believes, to
Jew first, then to Greek, for in it the justice of God is revealed from faith unto faith, as it is written: He who is
just lives by faith." The whole text is permeated with the
idea of the faith which brings salvation. But Luther was
obsessed with the idea of punitive justice; it had such a
strong hold on him that it dominated his thinking and was
in his mind before he looked at the text. He approached the
text with this idea and did not read the Scripture in such a
way as to be able to see the solution to his problems. This
illustrates again how incapable he was of going beyond
himself and simply taking the text as it stood—a text which
offered him as clearly as possible the very thing he was so
passionately seeking—the path to salvation.

Here again Luther tore the controverted point from the
whole context of Catholic doctrine and looked at only one
side. In a fully Catholic context of Thomas or Scotus, Luther's difficulty could not have arisen, because to Thomas
or Scotus, grace occupied the center of the stage and the
one-sided interpretation which limited the meaning of justice to the punitive variety would not have been possible.

That the point of departure of the Reformation was less
than fully Catholic is clear from another fact: Luther never
really understood the parable of the unprofitable servant;
he had eyes only for the Pauline theology of sin as it is
presented in the famous Chapter Seven of the Epistle to the
Romans. In this chapter, the doctrine is presented in as
strong a language as possible in order that the thought may
receive the emphasis it deserves. In addition, not all of
Paul's doctrine is contained in the Epistle and not all of the
doctrine of the Epistle is given in Chapter Seven. In
Luther's case, Paul's theology of sin was emphasized to the
point of exaggeration because of the intensity of his own

internal struggles and of his experience of sin. Luther had been driven to distraction by his doubts and this shows it. There is a great difference between Luther's concept of sin and the calm and earnest attitude of the servant mentioned in the synoptic Gospels, who, even when he had done everything (which, by the way, was what Luther was always trying to do) knew that he was still an unprofitable servant, but who knows at the same time that he is a child of God always living in and protected by the loving care of the Father.

Finally the question whether Luther was really on intimate terms with the spirit of Scripture has much light shed on it by another fact of his later life. Luther did not have a high opinion of the Epistle of St. James or the Apocalypse of St. John. In translating the New Testament, he did translate both of these books, but only rarely drew theological proofs from them. His basic attitude toward both books was expressed by his feeling that whoever could do anything with them was welcome to. He couldn't, because, in his words, they did not "treat of Christ." Above all, he had no esteem for the "insipid" Epistle of St. James, which, in the Second Chapter so definitely rejects faith without good works. As he put it: "Whoever can reconcile Paul and James, I'll give him my doctor's biretta and let myself be called a fool." His judgment of St. John's Apocalypse is revealing: "I will tell you what my feelings are; I cannot see the Holy Spirit at work in this book; I cannot give myself to this book."

Luther rebelled against the Church because he said it had tampered with the inviolable Word of God. Now we see Luther himself simply setting aside two whole books of the New Testament as unimportant. This is quite hard to

reconcile with his claim of complete devotion to the Word
of God.

If we consider all the elements of the New Testament
that are left out of Luther's doctrine (both at the time of
the definitive break with the Church and later on) and if
we keep in mind that he revolted against a Church which
alone had been looked on by all Western Christendom as
the source of eternal salvation, we would have reason to
say that Luther's claim to be guided entirely and solely by
Scripture was utterly unfounded. We are thus forced to the
conclusion that Luther was not receptive to the full message
of Scripture.

Luther's understanding of the full message of Scripture
was defective not only because of his failure to incorporate
all of Scripture into his teaching, insofar as certain sections of Scripture are strangely lacking, but also an oversimplification in which some of the essential aspects of the
message are left out. More of this, however, later.

Once this has been understood, we can agree with the
views of Professor Brandt who posed this objection. By
reducing all of revelation to the question of justification,
Luther did indeed hit on a central point, from which the
most important elements of the message of the New Testament proceed in logical order and from which they derive
their efficacy. If this is the meaning of receptivity to the
whole Scripture, then we agree that Luther was receptive.
However, this type of strict unity is nothing but an inadmissible tendency to a one-sided view which we must reject
as contrary to the spirit of Scripture.

The weakest aspect of Luther's doctrine was his exaggerated tendency to see justification as the sole content of
revelation. Christianity is salvation, but it contains a num-

ber of elements beyond an anthropocentrically conceived process of justification: adoration of the Father; the prayer, "Thy Kingdom come"; the revelation of the divine life which our Lord shares with His elect—all of these are essential elements of Christianity.

What were the discoveries made by Luther? Luther discovered the essence of Catholicism for himself but over-simplified it in such a way as to be led into heresy. We will have to be satisfied with a few indications of this, omitting much of the development and further precisions which could be made.

Luther's first point was that justification comes through faith alone. The Gospel message is realized in a personal, absolutely free encounter with God by sinful man whom He raised to Himself. On the side of man, his will as the result of original sin is utterly powerless to aid him in the process. God's approach is due entirely to the faith which He freely grants, and does not depend either on works or on the mediacy of a sacramental priesthood. Not only is the man who is justified also a sinner, but his sin is his justification.

Second: the Gospel, as its name suggests, is the proclamation of the good news of God, not the news of the divine wrath. In accordance with this conviction, Luther taught his distinctive doctrine of trust in God and a subjective conviction of salvation.

Because of this, the charge was made that he preached a superficial and ill-founded type of confidence, but such an interpretation is unjust to Luther. It is true that in his doctrine there are aspects of quietism that are dangerous. His paradoxical form of expression offers many difficulties and a tendency to offer rash solutions for every problem is perhaps the greatest source of danger. But there is an im-

portant fact on the other side of the ledger: at the time the
Reformation began, Luther's first thesis on indulgences
read as follows: "When our Lord Jesus Christ said 'Do
Penance,' He intended that the entire life of the Christian
should be an act of penance." This does not sound like the
advice of a pietist or quietist to "rest in the wounds of
Christ," and this remained a prime concern of Luther his
whole life long. In addition to his theology of confidence
and inseparable from it, Luther has a profound theology
of the Cross. Concerning his confidence in salvation, Luther rejects confidence entirely if it is superficial; confidence
in one's own salvation is guaranteed only by one's doubts.

Third: justification is realized not through an interior
transformation by means of infused grace; rather it is conceived in a purely ethical framework and the sacraments
are definitely pushed into the background.

Fourth: dogmatic traditions and the living magisterium
are neglected in ever-increasing measure and finally are
utterly rejected. For Luther there is only one source of the
faith—the word of God in Holy Scripture.

In making this bare enumeration, we must realize that,
though all of Luther's doctrine rests on a small number of
basic conceptions, it is not capable of being derived from
them. Different elements are always being developed by
Luther, with infinite variety. The further evolution of Luther's doctrine and his open battle with the Church were
strongly, even essentially, dependent on the rich variety of
religious experience and the tremendous earnestness with
which Luther took the question of religion.

In truth we should now try to see Luther as a man of
prayer; he was a man of prayer in a high degree. He wrote
a great number of prayers, he prayed easily, even in ordinary conversation. God was near him; for him, God was the

most proximate reality. If we read certain of Luther's polemic writings where he took issue with the theologians of the Church, often enough we note that the dogmatically correct writings of the Catholic lack real religious depth, while Luther's writings show that his attitude was basically prayerful. Luther showed that in his dispute with the Franciscan, Alfeld, on the *Salve Regina*. Luther's explanation of the *Magnificat* could, not too many years later, be incorporated into a valuable collection of Marian literature by a Catholic theologian.

Unfortunately, the variety and depth manifest in Luther's work is subject to great limitations. His lack of prudence and moderation, the unrestrained character of his formulations, and an impulsiveness often severely limit the value of what he has to say.

In addition, Luther gives a very inaccurate picture of the Church and the Papacy; there are direct and even grotesque misinterpretations that succeeding generations of Protestants who derived their ideas of the Catholic Church from Luther continued to hold to what we may call the Luther legend. This was inevitable, because from their own experience they knew little or nothing of the Church or of religious life; it was inevitable that they should believe the account given by the apparently competent individual who had been a monk. The picture of the papal Church that Luther handed on was full of errors to the point of caricature. The worst of these was the statement that he made any number of times and as bluntly as possible, that faith had been utterly perverted in the Roman Church and that only hypocrisy remained.

Today we no longer need to prove that Luther originated a true legend regarding the nature and doctrine of the Church. Protestant scholarship, as exemplified in the definitive conclusions reached by Otto Scheel, is in full accord with Catholic scholarship on this point.

Can we say that Luther was a liar? This is the conclusion preferred by generations of Catholic polemical writers from the time of the earliest disputes during the Reformation. This conclusion has been maintained up to our own day, partly because of a dependence on the Catholic theologians who first entered into the controversy and partly because of the facts themselves. This is not merely to be thought of as a thoroughly objectionable bit of ill-will. The objective falsehoods in Luther's works were great and frequent. He contradicted himself on so many occasions. He frequently showed so little reverence and humility in regard to events of the past and the doctrine of the Church that, for the type of analysis that could be made in the sixteenth, seventeenth, and eighteenth centuries, it was quite easy to arrive at the conclusion that Luther was a liar. In regard to a number of erroneous Catholic interpretations of Luther and his work, this must be said: Luther himself, in his words and in his manner of speaking, was to a great extent responsible for the misinterpretation.

Only modern times with their completely new science of historical method were able to penetrate beneath the surface. For this reason, the category *liar* is quite insufficient to explain the dialectical tensions in Luther which reach the point of contradicting our other sources, the facts themselves and his own assertions. There are some cases in Luther's life where in historically important matters he simply did not respect the truth. This is above all the case with the second marriage of Philip of Hesse. But on the whole, Luther was a truthful man. He was no liar. He wanted his words to be taken at face value. Remember what we said previously about the gradual process of development that Luther underwent and the substantial change that took place in him. In addition, in many of Luther's statements that seem to run directly counter to Catholic teaching, we have a clear echo of his Ockhamist point of departure which was not fully Catholic. Finally, we must take into account the all-pervading influence of the abuses current in the Church which to a significant extent simply escape our powers of imagination.

From the time of his lecture on the Epistle to the Romans (1515-16), we find Luther using rather strong language, and later on his condemnations of the monks, the pope, the Papists and the Mass tended to become sharp and crude. This crudity is most instructive for our understanding of the man, his work, and different aspects of his influence.

Certainly this coarseness is objectively intended and justified to a great extent. With Luther it was a question of a personal matter of conscience in a matter he regarded as of the highest importance. If he was really convinced that the pope was the Antichrist, then his condemnation could not be too sharp. In subjectively good faith he could apply to himself the words of Scripture: "The zeal of Thy house hath devoured me."

But often there was question not only of the objective opposition which Melanchthon pointed out in his funeral oration; in many cases we find that he did yield to impulsive hatred.

Luther could be utterly unrestrained in his abusiveness; he gave free rein to his abuse whether against well-known "official" enemies or against former friends like Agricola or Thomas More. Note that we are not trying to play the prude at Luther's expense. Luther was a peasant and much of the crudity he used in speaking and writing does serve

to open up a discussion, but there are other cases where
Luther just revels in the gutter; emotion takes over and
breaks all the bonds, indicating quite vividly Luther's lack
of moderation and restraint. His invective is not only dis-
armingly coarse, but shockingly unrestrained. Even when
not aiming at a specific opponent, he can be frightfully
blunt and shameless; the earthy vividness of his expression
simply knows no limits.

The worst feature is that this crudity often has an essential part in his religious discussions—sacred things are
touched with profane hands and we find a turgid mixture
of lofty religious sentiments and thoroughly coarse imagery.
There are pages in Luther's writings, pictures and verses
which simply cannot be justified—the reader involuntarily
shrinks back from them. They are simply unworthy, and
unfortunately provide impressive proof that Luther, the
champion of faith, the zealous man of prayer, who spoke
continually of the spirit of the Gospel, had simply not imbibed deeply of this spirit (cf. Erasmus *Diatribe* 18). He
did not rise to the level of sanctity. If in earlier days, Protestant writers regarded this old misunderstanding of Christian norms and this fruitless exaggeration of anti-Roman
sentiment as one of Luther's good qualities, it is an encouraging sign of the *metanoia* of our own day that now
both Protestants and Catholics are saddened by the events
we are discussing.

Ritter expressed the correct opinion that Luther's personality must be taken as a whole. Luther's objective rejection of the Church, his impulsiveness and crudity must
be studied in the context of the unity of Luther's own vital
personality. In many cases we find both elements combined;
but we can also put our finger on what is simply not objective, what is due to his impulsiveness and coarseness. To

the present day, an attempt has been made to justify Luther's excesses by pointing out that the entire sixteenth century was characterized by this crudity and that the Catholic polemical writers followed the same course. But this assertion is not entirely true. The climate of the age does relieve individuals of responsibility; this is as true of Luther as it is of Eck or Emser, but no one ever went as far as Luther in his well-known abusive characterizations, verses, and the like. Finally, if we look at Luther's emotional impulsiveness, it cannot be shown that any one of the Catholic polemical writers was motivated by burning hatred as Luther was.

That this coarseness has left an imprint on all of Luther's work is much more important than merely to depict the less attractive side of his character. To be sure, the excessive crudities indicate the presence of turbulent and irrational elements. These do not add to the authority of one who struggles for the pure word of God but actually cause tremendous difficulties in this area where sanctity should be found.

There is a more important consideration though. Luther's unbridled sallies are never merely external abuse, nor do they come by way of crude reaction to a situation; they are rooted objectively in Luther's own position. Thus it is that Luther adduces literally incredible monstrosities to justify his revolt against the Roman Church; his speeches and writings found their way in this form into the Protestant polemic literature and were used again and again to justify the separation from the mother church.

This is one of the main points on which the discussion between the Churches will hinge; Luther's own separation from the Church occurred after a period in which he grew away from the Church though still formally Catholic. In his open break patently unjust exaggerations played a major part and falsified facts, though they were taken quite seriously by Luther. The subsequent division of the sects with the passing years is essentially dependent on this deficient and unsatisfactory foundation.

A number of questions come to mind concerning Luther's pride and sense of superiority. The Catholic, especially the Roman, attitude toward the heretic tends to see in him one whose pride came before his fall. This judgment of Luther was made with special emphasis from the beginning, but as always exaggeration caused much harm. Distinctions must be made if truth is to be respected and if we are to realize a genuinely Catholic breadth of view.

Luther was quite emphatic about considering himself God's Evangelist, and he referred to his own concerns as God's concern. But when he does this, it is often in matters which he felt to be a binding matter of conscience. This is important because all of Luther's work bears the stamp of profound humility. He never tired of repeating that the doctrine was not his, and his doctrine certainly did not tend to ennoble or flatter man; it rather demands and asserts a negation of human powers.

When Luther died they found on his desk a tablet that contained probably the last words written by the Reformer. Uniting his thoughts with those of the Psalmist, he had written: "It is true that we are beggars. . . ." Coming as they do at the conclusion of such a violent life, these words do not point in the direction of pride.

Of course there is another side. It is not as simple as Harnack put it when he said that Luther's pride consisted solely in the fact that his emotional drive was stronger than that of other men. He was impulsive and often showed that he was acutely conscious of his own powers. Although Lu-

ther was a man of genius, endowed with great gifts of intellect and will, in Luther's actions and words the fine line
that separates zeal for the Lord's house from emphatic
defense of his own position was often crossed. Here we find
once more the essential problem of the relationship between
the will and the objective order fundamental in any assessment of Luther. Things were never as Luther really wanted
them to be.

We might make an attempt to understand this difficult
and delicate matter by a comparison of Luther with St.
Francis of Assisi. Our purpose is not to make an odious
comparison between Luther's earthy approach and the
transparent sanctity of Francis. My readers will appreciate
from the general tenor of the book so far that such partisan
zeal can have no place here. What will we do then? We
study two gifted personalities, both of whom had an influence that has lasted for centuries, both of whom had
within them the sources of their own development, both of
whom were profoundly convinced that they were engaged
in God's work. To prove our point in Francis's case, we
need merely recall the section of his *Testament* where he
emphasized so pointedly *"Deus revelavit mihi. . . ."* Not
just any teacher, but God Himself had formed him. Again,
look at the tremendous powers Francis put to work: every
aspect of his activity was thoroughly subject to the service
and will of God. It is quite clear that Luther's emotional,
acquisitive, and peremptory way of acting is worlds apart
from this attractive style which Francis manifests.

This summary of Luther's objective attitude and the
problems of the relation of his will to the real order, lead
us to some final conclusions on Luther. We have sufficiently
seen that Luther's actions were extremely violent and unre-

strained and that he relied too much on himself alone. Then, surveying his whole life and seeking for the ultimate causes, we come again and again to the same grave deficiency in Luther's intellectual and spiritual outlook: over-development of the subjective and personal elements that tended toward real subjectivism. (Incidentally we have in Luther a prototype of the subjectivism that has been such a threat in our modern age and has wrought such havoc in Germany. More of this later.)

What precisely does the word *subjectivistic* mean when applied to Luther? I certainly am not taking the word in the sense of an autonomous or arbitrary approach as it was used in the eighteenth and even more in the nineteenth and twentieth centuries. Luther was still powerfully influenced by tradition. In spite of everything we have said about his independence of tradition, he never affirms a rational or rationalistic, an unhistorical or fanatic independence of what his Catholic forbears had achieved. He never, for example, intended to secularize divine service as Zwingli did; he never rallied to the side of the fanatics. Above all, he felt that he was bound to the *Word* of Holy Scripture. This tendency is so strong that we could probably speak in his case of an objective subjectivism or, if one prefers, a subjective objectivism.

In spite of this, his fundamental assertions are dominated by the subjective element; for Luther there was no living magisterium—in the last analysis he had only the conscience of the individual faced with the word of Scripture. In addition he excluded the objective sacramental element to a marked degree.

Everything Luther said bore the imprint of his extraordinary and dangerous individualism that we have so often

mentioned. We found in all the public utterances the subjective and personal element is always coming to the fore
as a distinct trait of Luther.

Luther's own struggle in religious life was not aimed
primarily or in any noteworthy sense at the honor and glory
of God or the coming of His kingdom. It was concerned
solely with the problem of salvation, quite narrowly limited
to the salvation of one soul—Luther's own. To be sure,
Luther's piety is theocentric in the profound sense we used
in referring to him as a religious man; but the all-important
struggle to find a merciful God was not waged for the sake
of fulfilling the divine will, but for his own salvation. The
zeal for the spread of the Kingdom was a later addition; the
distraught monk was not too interested in this aspect.

The spiritual life of Luther in later years shows the
same subjective tendencies. Preuss called it, "a significant
turn in the history of Christian piety that Luther esteemed
real prayer of petition above the pure prayer of adoration." [1]
He made much of the fact that for Luther, faith was less
a free gift than a strong grasping of Christ to secure one's
own salvation.[2] But the Protestant theologian Echternach
points to the fact that we have here an indication of dangerously subjective tendencies: "Isn't the scope of religion expressly directed to man and because of this choice, Lutheranism given a character that may ultimately destroy it?" [3]

In his pamphlet, "Luther from the Catholic Point of
View" (Bonn, 1946), Johannes Hessen tries, in a somewhat *a priori* framework to disprove the arguments which
point to Luther's subjective tendencies by regarding him as
a prophet.

[1] *Luther, Der Christenmensch,* p. 20.
[2] *Op. cit.,* p. 139.
[3] *Th. L. Zt.* 44, p. 33.

Now it is generally recognized that Luther was a representative of the prophetic type, but if we are to draw valid conclusions from this fact, the concept must be made more exact, i.e., based on the events of Luther's life. For this reason we must say that Luther was not a prophet in the sense in which we apply the word to those who spoke the word of God in the Old Testament. Whenever the Old Testament prophets announced what God had revealed to them, it was, so to speak, a "first edition." They announced a *new* revelation, something previously essentially unknown. With Luther, the case was entirely different. He neither wished nor was able to be anything but the Evangelist of the divine will which had been publicly and definitively revealed for a long time. Luther did not appeal to a private revelation; his message was not: "Thus spake the Lord," but "Thus it is written." The content of Luther's preaching was always subject to control: this was in fact his goal and stood in sharp contrast to the categorical demands of the prophetic element of his character. His goal was to measure his doctrine by the word of Scripture. For Luther, the only thing that counted was that in extent and intent his preaching should conform to the Gospel. If he did not attain that goal and erred in his interpretation due to the limitations imposed on the message by his own personality and the excessive introversion that was part of it, then without doubt this development of the Gospel message along the lines of his own personal bent merits the name of individualism and subjectivism.

Perhaps I should say a word about Luther's famous statement: "*pecca fortiter.*" In this statement as in his other, "It is of no great significance that we commit serious sin," we have an example of a dangerous rashness that marks not only Luther's formulation of a view, but his position itself.

He thought and spoke in an undisciplined way. Ideas so formulated create great danger that those who do not share Luther's religious concern will find in them an excuse for letting themselves go in religious and moral matters. Without doubt, Luther's words often had this effect. The same thing happened when Luther preached so strongly his doctrine of faith alone without good works. Luther did not leave the slightest doubt that a Christian life which does not express itself in good works would be nothing but a hollow lie. Yet he cannot be exonerated of the charge that a number of people without any ill will interpreted his doctrine in a very lax sense. He was too careless in his manner of speaking and his point of departure was too negative. This is quite evident when we compare Luther's phrase, "*pecca fortiter*" with St. Augustine's, "love and do what you will!" Augustine presupposed the close connection of the moral order with faith; this was his starting point. The lack of this connection was one of the greatest deficiencies of Luther's work. Thus from the beginning of the Reformation to our own day, Luther's doctrine could be falsely interpreted as Bernard Shaw did in one of his serious moments: "One might say of him that he abolished the admission price to heaven." [4]

I feel that I should interpose a warning here. Since we began to speak of Luther as a religious man, we discussed many of the man's deficiencies and weaknesses; we were forced to deny that his basic decisions were justified. But now we must take to heart what I said at the beginning: we must be willing to look at both sides of the picture. Despite all that we have said, Luther was a great and fervent believer, filled with the faith that moves mountains. He burned with love for the Lord Jesus and his zeal for preaching the Gospel was unquenchable.

[4] *Die Neue Rundschau,* 1926, p. 627.

Despite all the important statements one might make of Luther and his work, in the final analysis, the result of his life and work was a negative one, a schism within Christendom. To be sure, it was the Church that passed judgment on Luther and expelled him. It was the Church that would not tolerate Luther in her midst, but that was merely the completion of the process that Luther had begun, while still in the Church. In the critical doctrines of importance, he no longer recognized the Catholic Church and her tenets. Separation from the Church was not easy, but after it came about, Luther contradicted a number of clear statements that he formerly had made. In his lecture on the Psalms (about 1512), he had said: "Unless doctrine can be authoritatively guaranteed by one living man, there will be as many doctrines as there are men." And as late as 1519, in the disputations at Leipzig, Luther had defended the position that not even God could give one the right to separate from the Roman Church. But he did finally separate himself from the Church, and in the consequent division of Christendom he found much to condemn.

In the thirties, Luther often gave expression to his pessimistic views about the confusion that would follow his death. Capito, in 1538, had the following to say: "The Lord is showing us now how much harm we have done with our overzealous attack against the Papacy. Since we have eliminated the Pope, the ministry of the Word, the sacraments, and pastoral care have come to nought. The people cry out, 'I understand the Gospel well enough; I can read it myself. Why do I need your help? Preach to those who want to listen to you and let them accept what they want.' "

Subjectivism had begun to prevail. In a perfectly logical fashion, the chasm became ever wider, by bringing out more and more divisions and by leading to a denial of the

basic positions of the Reformation as envisaged by Luther.
We will consider this more fully in subsequent chapters.

We come not to a new consideration: How were Luther's ideas and demands put into practice? Was the spread
of the Reformation due solely to the religious dynamism
it created? The importance assigned to the causes of the
Reformation confirmed the fact that religious and spiritual
forces alone were not responsible for the Reformation.
Many non-religious and irreligious elements were involved
in bringing this about. This particularly applies to the historical development or the process of the Reform itself. It
would constitute an unjust and foolish prejudice to refuse
to see in the amazingly rapid success of the Reformation a
true sense of religious earnestness and a genuine power of
conviction because these elements were undoubtedly present, although frequently less important than political and
economic considerations.

The ideas of the "pure Word of God," and an "absolutely binding conscience," and the "freedom of the Christian," were quite often perverted. P. W. Fuchs, who investigated quite thoroughly the effects of the reform preaching
on the Peasants' Rebellion, has this to say, "It must be
stated that in both towns and countryside the Reformation
prevailed amid scenes of violence." [5] We need not examine
all of the facts individually, but merely remember the complaints of Luther and Melanchthon against the egoism of
the princes. Luther's inflammatory preaching had itself
opened up the floodgates. The peasants remembered more
his scornful disregard of the princes than they did his
warnings; they remembered only his threats, "People will
not and cannot tolerate your malice and your tyranny for
long."

Negotiations held in the assemblies and the practical

[5] *Welt als Geschichte,* 1941, 90.

application of the norm, *cuius regio, eius religio,* offer cogent proof that the new doctrine spread amid scenes of violence. The conclusion is evident: Were it not for the selfishness of the Church authorities in rural districts, and the ecclesiastical power of town governments, Luther might have appeared, but the Reformation would not have succeeded.

We conclude with a brief summary. During the period preceding the Reformation the Church, particularly the higher clergy, and much of the contemporary theology, were in dire need of radical criticism; this made the Reformation a historical necessity. This is quite evident from the fact that the struggle of the Church against the Reformation was in large measure carried on in a manner and with means that were not religious. Thus the Reformation becomes a Catholic concern insofar as Catholics must share responsibility and guilt for bringing it about.

Martin Luther, the immediate cause of the Reformation, in the process of resolving his profound struggles of conscience, left the Church although he had not previously intended to do so. For this action the Catholic theology of the day must bear a great deal of the blame. Throughout these events Luther appears as a thoroughly religious man who drew great inspiration from the Bible and shared this with others.

Luther's theology of confidence in God and of man's certitude of salvation, has in the sense in which Luther intended them, nothing to do with superficial indifference. Luther's whole doctrine on this point is characterized by an absolute seriousness proper to the Christian in such matters.

Luther's whole disposition tended toward subjectivism and made him see all in a rather one-sided way.

Luther's separation from the Church was a gradual rejection of those elements in his thinking and his point of view that were not thoroughly Catholic.

Luther's interpretation of the Bible was profoundly conditioned by his own personality, likes, and dislikes.

Luther justified his struggle against the Church by giving an essentially erroneous picture of Catholic doctrine which was passed on by tradition to later generations of Protestants.

The conclusion that must be drawn is extremely serious. If Luther left the Church because he misunderstood the true Catholic doctrine, and if he gave his followers an essentially false picture of what Catholic doctrine was, then first of all, we must deny that he had any real justification for leaving the Church, and secondly, the false picture must be replaced by a true one.

Thus it means that it was wrong for Catholics and Protestants to divide, to separate, in the first place. At the same time our true positions are seen to be incomparably closer to one another than we had suspected. In the next two chapters we will investigate these points in much greater detail.

If we take these conclusions seriously, we must come face to face with the situation mentioned in the First Chapter. At that time we asked the question: If the Reformation came about because of misunderstanding and false presuppositions, can we in conscience permit the separation to continue? I feel that this question is more immediate and demanding now than previously. If we truly deserve the name of Christians, there is no time for hesitation or delay. As Christians, all of us have a serious obligation to consider anew the task of the Reformation. It is clear that in our own day this is not only possible but offers much hope of success. Here again we must emphasize even more strongly that the most powerful means at our disposal is prayer. The Reformation has influenced the destiny of the entire world to our own day. It is precisely in our own day that the real meaning of the Reformation is becoming understood more clearly once again. What can we do in the face of the massive threat that we see before us, the *mysterium iniquitatis,* which causes love and faith to grow cold and makes men deaf to the message of the one Lord of the one Church? We can do nothing better than invoke the aid of God Himself by prayer.

What I have said before, I must repeat: this prayer of union in faith is not something that we may make or omit as we please; it is our *duty*. We must make a firm resolution to do everything in our power to spread an understanding of this fact among those with whom we come into contact.

III

Reform within
the Church in the
Sixteenth Century

The history of the sixteenth century is dominated by the Reformation and rightly so, for the Reformation was the most important event of the century. It remains important in our own day because of the influence it has exerted on the destiny of the entire world. It is important in a special way to Catholics for, as we have seen, it is a Catholic concern.

The Reformation concerns Catholics in another sense of the word, for the Catholic reform of the sixteenth century can be regarded as a product of the Protestant Reformation. For centuries the cry for reform in head and members had been raised in vain. Luther's revolt finally forced men to heed this cry, just as it gradually brought to an end the influence of certain destructive tendencies, such as the cultural religion of the humanists. The regeneration of the Church came about only after Luther's revolt.

Of its nature an historical process at any given moment will exhibit characteristics that are not only diverse, but from the purely logical point of view, contradictory. History has all of the fullness, complexity, and richness of life; no logical principle nor sum of principles can encompass its rich variety. History is complex. The quality regarded as most characteristic of a period is a sum of the elements characterizing it, even though some may be contradictory. It is never a single element; no historical period or development can be characterized from a single point of view.

After the year 1520, the sixteenth century was not an age of contrasts in a classical sense in which we found the fifteenth century. Yet the events of the sixteenth century, so rich and varied, to some extent, as we previously said, offer a number of contrasts quite applicable to the history of the Church during this century.

The Reformation was not the only event of importance in the sixteenth century; for Catholics it was not the event of most importance. Nevertheless it is true that in the mind of the average person, understandably and justifiably, this century is most noteworthy for the Reformation, Luther, and the other reformers—all of which marked the birth of a new era of world history. The stress placed on the importance of the Reformation should not make us blind to the fact that during this same century a great deal of activity took place within the framework of the Church itself. This activity, extending beyond a Counter Reformation, was the more important development. Thus, in fact, a third element between the Reformation and the Counter Reformation arose: reform within the Church.

To say that this reform within the Church was in a proper sense a manifestation of the life of the Church of the time is to see that the forces involved were primarily and essentially independent of the Reformation. We assert that, in spite of the undeniable importance of Luther's reform for the rebirth of the Church, the rebirth itself was the result of forces essentially independent of the Reformation, in existence before the Reformation, and continually active during the Reformation. These influences originated entirely apart from the sphere of the Reformation and its interests. These assertions can be proven only by describing the actual course of the reform within the Church.

In the study of human history, that is, in the interpretation of a vital historical process, a healthy distrust of conclusions is a great asset. This is particularly true if historical statements touch upon vital areas of human religious interests, such as those concerning the Reformation, especially in Germany. This is more important when statements are made in connection with the unity movements of the Churches which is of such significance to us in our times.

The attitude that forms the basis of discussions must be that our only concern is to speak the truth in charity. History does not belong to us but to God, for it is His work; our task is to see His hand in it. When we mentioned in the second chapter that the Catholic should be able to accept the truth even if it is not pleasant or flattering, we hope we have the right to expect that our Protestant brethren will face the truth as honestly when we speak of developments which favor the Catholic position. If in discussing the present topic a sense of pride or enthusiasm arises among Catholics, these emotions must not be allowed to degenerate into a feeling of self-satisfied superiority. This will be easier if we recall that there were unattractive aspects of the great reform within the Church. We must remember that the process of decay that provoked the protest of the Christian conscience was already far advanced. In point of fact, the seeds of dissolution, which we termed the causes of the Reformation, the lack of theological clarity, the substitution of humanistic for religious values—all made it difficult to remedy the situation in a short time, particularly since these defects were not merely accidental deviations due to ill will or the moral weaknesses of individuals. They were, instead, intimately dependent on constitutive elements of

the life of the medieval Church, particularly manifested in
the mutual interdependence of the Church and the world
and in a medieval clericalism in which the clergy constituted an economically and socially preferred class. These
elements, which gave rise to difficulties at the end of the
Middle Ages with a certain logical or even historical necessity, were not eliminated in either the sixteenth or seventeenth century. They remained important aspects in the life
of the Church until the time of the French Revolution.

The rather thorough disorder of ecclesiastical life at the
end of the Middle Ages made improvements effected by
reform within the Church fragmentary, slow of progress,
or utterly ineffective. At times they threatened to fall back
into the mire from which they had come. In Germany, even
after 1570, many attempts at reform were struggling against
the same conditions of moral and spiritual weakness that
characterized the fifteenth and early part of the sixteenth
centuries. The same period saw forces growing active within
the Church over several decades which would be responsible for much success in the reform of the Church.

We have already noted the sad truth that on three different occasions the Reformation was kept alive because
of the acts of a pope which sacrificed religious interests for
political ones. We must also recall that the last time that
this occurred, Pope Paul III had already been occupied
with the problems of reform for more than a decade. In
addition it is well not to forget that many weaknesses of
ecclesiastical life continued not only to the end of the sixteenth century but through to the seventeenth century, one
in many respects so glorious for the Church and one in
which the forces of disorder were by no means so exten-
sively active. Though we have words of high praise for the
reform within the Church, we cannot indulge in unhistor-

ical, useless, or confused generalizations. We have no desire to paint a bright picture that avoids facing any of the real problems; we cannot yield to the temptation of stressing one or two disquieting elements without taking into account true failures on the Catholic side.

It is equally true that both persistent evils and a constant danger of relapse indicate the vast scope of the problems and the magnitude of achievement in their solutions. No natural explanation exists for the manner in which the Church disposed of the poison which had infected it and thus brought about its own rejuvenation in a way that led to a true transformation throughout the world.

An objective study of these facts is extremely difficult for Protestant Christians, especially in Germany. Impressed by the tremendous events of the Reformation in Germany, they have eyes for the life of the Church there alone, but pay too little attention to events outside their native land, and simply cannot evaluate their true worth in any discussions. The Church is supranational, a quality belonging to its very nature. Although it is true and necessary that within the Church particular characteristics of each nation must be taken into account, yet the unity of the Church in all nations comprising it needs an even greater emphasis. The Church is one body, essentially the same in Italy, France, or England; all of its members are in an essential, mutual, spiritual dependence on one another in a communion of saints. This one body suffers as a whole in the weakness of one member; the special vitality of one member works to the advantage of the whole.

The only way to view the Church which does justice to its nature is to respect the essential relationships between all members, all its geographical and physical parts. The only way to get a balanced view of the situation in Germany is to look at the entire Church and take into account all of the forces and developments involved throughout the whole Church.

In Germany in the sixteenth and seventeenth century the forces of reform within the Church were relatively weak; this cannot obscure the fact, however, that the Church as a whole went through a period of great rejuvenation at that time.

In the natural course of developments, the separatist and revolutionary elements of the Reformation were most vital in those areas where the Reformation enjoyed its greatest success. The Protestant Reformation, as a germanic development, was immediately responsible for the exhausting wars between the churches. Thus it is easy to understand why and how the vitality of the Church in Germany was weakened and why the Church in the Latin countries was incomparably more healthy and creative than in the germanic areas in general.

Actually, reform within the Church during the sixteenth century came predominantly from the countries of southern Europe, especially Spain and Italy. Post-Reformation Catholicism bears a strong Latin imprint. This presented certain disadvantages from the German point of view and has remained something of a difficulty right up to the present day. It is a form of penance immanent in the historical process which is imposed on the German people for the fact that the Reformation came from their section of the Church.

However, the fact that Catholicism bears a predominantly Latin imprint is a loss for the entire Church and deprives it of real strength; Germany's contribution to the life of the whole Church was not enough, for the German

Catholic consciousness itself was insufficiently strong. Rome's distrust of things German has never been completely overcome. These are and should be top-priority questions in Germany. They can be solved with the aid of natural means according to the principle that grace builds on nature. There is a solid foundation for asking the indulgence of Rome regarding the solution of certain religious and ecclesiastical problems in Germany. For Germany is not only the land of the Reformation; it is also the country that decisively saved the Papacy, in the tenth century and later restored its unity at the beginning of the fifteenth century through the Emperor Sigismund. The influence of medieval Germany on the formation of the Latin liturgy and the Christianization of the East was of primary importance. In addition the example of Pope Pius XII often showed how much understanding the Germans as children of the Church might find in Rome.

Let us, however, not be too ready to accept this rather plausible solution. In discussing the cause of the Reformation we found that the appalling corruption afflicting the Church was perhaps greatest right in the Rome of the Renaissance popes. Actually life had become not as paganized in Germany as in Italy at that time. For despite the radical humanism of the Erfurt school the utterly pagan lack of restraint in the pursuit of the joys of this life was never as prominent as in Italy, even at the papal court. The simoniacal deals made in Rome were merely used to advantage in Germany. St. Clement Mary Hofbauer expressed it quite clearly: "The Reformation came because of the basic need of the German people for real piety." If that is true, then it is easy to see why Germany contributed so little to the reform within the Church and why the Latin countries offered so much. Facts of such supreme importance must humbly be acknowledged by every Catholic; each must be ready to admit his own guilt.

This, however, does not penetrate to the central core of the matter. In speaking of weaknesses within the Church, I strongly emphasized that the moral element was never really the decisive factor in the religious life of the Church during any given period. The truth of the fundamental principles on which a given age is structured makes the difference. Moral guilt of the worst type does not constitute the greatest evil that can afflict the Church at any time; far worse are doctrinal deviations that make it impossible to remedy a moral evil. These questions touch upon the ultimate difference between the subjective evaluation of a phenomenon and its objective reality, a difference between two fundamentally different ways of looking at the world—the Germanic and the Latin. In other words we are dealing with a problem of form.

In Germany, Luther, driven by the inexorable demands of his own conscience, touched upon the very principles from which the life of the Church flows. In a thoroughly subjectivist way he picked and chose from among them: the magisterium, sacramental priesthood, the principle that the effect of the sacrament was independent of the one who administered it, the sacrifice of the Mass—all these disappeared. It was precisely Luther's profound but dangerous overemphasis on faith that threatened the reality of Christian life with a dependence on subjective attitudes and conscience. (In this way Luther's doctrine was later deprived of all its content.)

In Italy, men had so given themselves to the pursuit of the joys of this life that grave harm was done to the communication of the Christian message; their unchristian lives were a caricature of the faith they professed. But the objective structure of the Church remained untouched; no one had real doubts concerning the magisterium, dogma, the priesthood, the efficacy of the sacraments. In the last analysis, despite all the violent criticism that can be heaped upon them, men in Italy had a real feeling for essential form, shared more deeply in the wisdom of history. They learned the lessons taught them by a centuries-long tradition. People knew or at least guessed that an appreciation of the values of the tradition was worth much more than an acceptance of even the best insights of an individual conscience.

In Italy, the surface had dried up and was desolate. But in the depths of the earth, the springs had not dried up and at any given moment under the impetus of a stronger flow from their subterranean sources, they could rise to the surface and once more irrigate the desolate land, changing the face of the arid landscape.

Thus it was that loyalty to the Church was the most profound element in the rebirth of the Church—loyalty to the Church despite all of the terrible deficiencies she exhibited in that day. This loyalty to the Church was richly blessed.

In our previous chapters we considered the events of struggle and strife in which Luther and the Reformation disrupted the pattern of life violently and thereby created a revolution that rocked the whole of Europe. So true was this that even today we experience a certain disquiet in studying Luther and his times for they still involve matters of ultimate concern to us.

Yet when we turn our attention to reform within the Church, we find a quite different story. In place of violent disruption of the old order brought on by the sudden outbreak of the religious revolution, we find a calm and restrained internal preparation for laborious undertakings and advances.

I have noted before that Catholic reform was faced with many obstacles and its progress was not uniform. In addition the complex series of events that we term a reform within the Church in the sixteenth century involved many areas, both geographical and spiritual. Since the inner significance of these events and the period in which they became manifest can be subject to no general law, a neat summary of the phenomenon is almost impossible. In addition, there has been too little investigation of the sources and the relative independence of the various manifestations of this reform within the Church.

On the other hand it is possible, without doing violence to the complexity of the events, to say that reform within the Church did manifest a certain recognizable rhythm and stages of development with an intrinsic bond to one another. For our purposes, we can divide these stages into a preparation, turning point, and completion.

Before our brief examination of the structure of the reform within the Church, we want to draw the attention of the reader to an historical event which not only overshadowed this development at the time, but in many respects furthered it—the sack of the city of Rome in 1527. It shocked an age and ended forever the splendid and sinful Rome of the Renaissance. It was, and was recognized as a judgment on the Renaissance Papacy. Its effects were not immediately apparent for life continued at the papal court much as before; yet the break had been made and could not long be ignored. The spirit of Savonarola's inspired call for penance hovered over the ruins. The frightful destruction of worldly Rome by the soldiers of the Imperial Army left its mark on the consciousness of the men of the age. With the year 1527 the Renaissance was definitely over. There was a profound change in the attitudes of men in society in general but especially in the Church. New attitudes and possibilities opened up for the Church. How they were employed determines our view of the whole period.

Naturally the true import of the sack of Rome can be grasped only if we do not consider it as an isolated event. It must be viewed together with the tremendous unrest of the fifteenth century; the fact that men were waiting for the end of the old age and the birth of the new; the disquieting influence of humanism and the Renaissance; the experience of so many perversions in the life of the Church and, as a reaction, the penitential preaching and attempts at reform in the fifteenth century, particularly by Savanarola; the events included in the phrase, "Luther and the Reformation," that had been making an increasing impression on Rome for nine years by this time—all of these events form the background of the sack of Rome in 1527.

At the very outset of our discussion of reform within the Church in the sixteenth century, we return to our original thesis: reform within the Church was basically not the result of the Protestant Reformation but a development drawing its inspiration from within the Church itself. The preparatory stages of this reform are nothing but the sum of many important and even significant reform movements of the late Middle Ages, the fifteenth century, a period preceding the Reformation.

Savonarola (†1499) is worthy of profound analysis to discover the biblical, theological, and ascetical traditions on which he was dependent. He can be viewed as the expression or the incarnation of the best attempts at reform in the fifteenth century. He was an example of the monastic life, characterized by prayer, sacrifice, penance, and devotion to the sacraments—all ordered to a profoundly pastoral concern for the cloister and the world, and concretized in a striking personality who was endowed with a great consciousness of his mission. A thoroughgoing reform might have begun with Savonarola, had it not been for his involvement in politics, especially since his opponent was Pope Alexander VI.

There were other great penitential preachers of the fifteenth century as well as thoroughgoing movements of reform in the older religious orders in all of the countries of Europe. The revival of strict observance of rule in the Augustinians, Franciscans, Dominicans, Carmelites, and Benedictines played a rôle in laying the foundations of reform within the Church.

Devotio moderna, mentioned in connection with the following of Christ at the end of the first chapter, is also an important part of this picture, for it represented a sincere attempt to take both prayer and the Christian life seriously. German mysticism of the late medieval period must also be studied to understand the positive religious forces still active within the German lands. The whole heritage of Christian art was part of the picture, as well as the truly humanistic piety of the Carthusians, particularly in their German foundations. All of these forces were operative in the new age of the Church which was on the horizon. We should also take note of the reform tendencies which cropped up from time to time at the Papal Curia itself. In fact, so loud was the clamor for reform in head and members that even in the time of Alexander VI a reform Bull got as far as the preparatory draft stage, in which this Pope pointed out that as a Cardinal under Pius II, Paul II, Sixtus IV and Innocent VIII he had worked for reform. The attempts at reform of the Fifth Lateran Council at the beginning of that century give some idea of the forces at work even though its decrees were never put in force. Neither can we forget the initiative shown by a large number of zealous bishops, among whom there were some truly outstanding persons. For example, the activity of Ximenes in Spain (†1517) was of inestimable value because of his own personal piety, the reform movements he began among the regular and the diocesan clergy, and his zeal for learning and for the missions.

Although none of these varied efforts succeeded nor were creative in the strict sense of the word and although they remained quite scattered, they were not in vain. These forces prepared the ground and, although they disappeared, they did so as the seed which must first die before the true growth can follow. When the time came and more powerful forces came into play, these earlier currents were integrated into the great stream which became the movement of reform within the Church. We have proof of this in a number of events which preceded and contributed to the Church's own renaissance. However we must be aware of the fact that not all of the events which contributed to revival and renewal can be isolated and analyzed, for we are dealing with a process of spiritual growth and development, where the precise relations of cause and effect are by no means so clear as they are in the sphere of the natural sciences. Movement of the human spirit is much more complex so that much in its development will necessarily elude us. This is nothing more than the great mystery of growth. We are aware of the forces set in motion and from the success of these we can draw legitimate conclusions about their origins.

If our study aimed at being exhaustive we would have

to restrict ourselves to the rôle of southern Europe in reform within the Church, because Germany's involvement in laying the ultimate foundations of reform was of greater importance than her immediate contribution to the Catholic revival. This involved, as I mentioned before, the *devotio moderna,* the new piety of the Carthusians, on which the Jesuits depend, the German reformers Busche and Coelde, and, perhaps most important of all, the work of Nicolaus of Cusa in the first half of the fifteenth century. The reform movements within the religious orders and the foundation of reform congregations also involved the German provinces of these orders to a significant degree. But this not really our concern, because the direct and organized preparation which led to renewal within the Church came from southern Europe, primarily from Spain and Italy. France later became a factor in the sixteenth century and an important one in the seventeenth.

It is in Spain that we first see the process of renewal at work. The late Middle Ages did not find the decay in Spain that existed in the rest of Europe. Spanish humanism of the fifteenth century, under the leadership of the gifted and pious Ximenes, is profoundly Christian and Church-orientated. In fact the whole fifteenth century humanistic revival in Spain remained true to the Church. The faith in Spain thus became the Catholicism of the future, endowed with tremendous vitality, as evidenced in Theresa of Avila (†1582), the Spanish theologians of the Council of Trent, and the ecclesiastical policy of Philip II, a vitality which, in its own sphere, began and carried to a successful conclusion the whole work of renewal and reform.

In Italy, the land of ecclesiastical, papal and curial decadence, the tide was turned and the most immediate impetus given to the ideals of reform.

At first glance the picture in Italy seems clear enough, but developments were really quite surprising. We have to remember, first of all, that the reform tendencies were very widespread in the Church, although the extent of their vitality and mutual dependence varied greatly, so that the foundations of reform within the Church cannot be traced to any single series of events of greater or lesser import. Rather the whole Church came gradually to breathe the atmosphere of reform, a gradual awareness of its need, that finally influenced the external structure of ecclesiastical life. The events that concern us now developed with more or less success as a part of this process.

If we keep all this in mind and realize that ultimately the reform of the clergy was the most important factor in the total reform, then we can say, without too much danger of oversimplification, that the most important factor in preparing the way for reform became the many confraternities which developed in the Middle Ages, more or less on the fringes of the official Church organization with a negligible dependence on the hierarchy. In Italy the most important of all these organizations was the Oratory of Divine Love. These independent organizations existed under this or similar names in various cities.

The Oratory of Divine Love in Rome was one of the many small groups which found laymen, priests, diplomats, humanists, doctors, and artists gathered together for the sake of mutual spiritual assistance. This assistance usually took the form of informal discussions in which both lay and clerical members took part on an equal basis—without any trace of clericalism in the bad sense. The whole purpose of the group was, quite simply, to grow in the love of God. Thus they emphasized a theme which was to develop such important and outstanding manifestations in the sixteenth and seventeenth centuries. The groups were not, as Ranke thought, primarily literary societies with a religious flavor, but basically religious in purpose. In such confraternities, every member had to take part in the discussions. We know that among others Machiavelli was a member and that one of his contributions was a meditation on the *De Profundis*. (According to Kaegi, Machiavelli never left the Church.)

These Oratories, such as existed in Vicenza, Verona, Brescia, and Genoa in the last decade of the fifteenth century and in Rome from the year 1517, developed their specific character when faced with the phenomenon of corruption and decay in the Church. They reacted not with bitter criticism or violent polemics, but rather with a program of self-sanctification and loyalty to the Church. For them, adherence and loyalty to the Church, a life of vital dependence on the Church, became an obvious necessity and a conscious goal. They took part in the Church's worship and received the sacraments regularly, for it was to be through this process of self-sanctification that they aimed at renewing the Church. To an age whose prime values were power and pleasure, they reaffirmed the worth of humility and abnegation. Although humanists, they did not overestimate the natural powers of man, but made God the total object of their hope and love. They were equally committed to cultivating the love of neighbor, again foreshadowing in this area the leading rôle that charity would play in the coming internal reform of the Church.

There was nothing earth-shaking about such a program; many of its individual elements were and are present at all times in the Church. It might seem strange that such a program or movement could be the source of profound ecclesiastical revival. The secret remains the same for any renewal or renaissance in either a secular or ecclesiastical society: a definite ideal is taken seriously and carried through to its ultimate conclusions. This means quite simply that in the modest beginnings represented by the confraternities, we encounter true holiness, at least in its initial stages. We see that no matter how intensively the members of the group strove for this desired goal, they were far from any program of busy hustling; they possessed, instead, a deep grasp of the mystery of growth and the respect in which it must be held.

Naturally not all members, either of the Roman Confraternity of Divine Love or of similar organizations in other cities, were of noteworthy sanctity, but in the Roman confraternity, we encounter two personalities who show quite clearly how the reform movement was to begin. Both were radical in their conception of reform and organized and carried through their program in the spirit of a true following of Christ. The sanctity of these men was not merely a general, undetermined form but possessed quite specific characteristics, exemplified in the persons of Gaetano da Thiene (†1547) and Gian Petro Carafa, who later became Pope Paul IV (1555-1559). Two more different personalities could not be imagined, but in this fact an indication of the contrasting forces that were needed for the work of purgation and reconstruction can be found. Gaetano was another St. Francis, a man of peace who would transform the world through love. Carafa was a fiery Neapolitan, harsh to the point of violence. Both were men of heroic abnegation, in whom we find total commitment to the Christian life, even though, to tell the truth, in Carafa, this total commitment at times was shocking and even destructive. In passing, we should note that in all truly creative unions the union is never monolithic; differences remain, as remain they must in any organism which is truly alive.

In the face of the tremendous amount of work involved in the transformation of the life of the Church, the influence of a few loosely organized confraternities and of men whose vocations were those of the ordinary walks of life in the world was not enough. Sooner or later this fact had to be grasped. To give the reform movement stability and permanence there had to be a complete transformation in the life of the clergy. To secure this goal of central importance, a religious order was needed. This need was filled by the Clerks Regular Theatine. The principal goal and achievement of this Order, which was to give more than two hundred bishops to the Church, had been recognized as essential for centuries: the practice of a truly apostolic life on the part of the clergy.

The principal obstacle to this end was the pursuit of possessions, money, and pleasure which seemed to be regarded as a hallmark of the clergy. The new order, therefore, was characterized by its emphasis on poverty; its members were quite serious about trusting their Father in heaven for everything. The Order as such owned nothing, and not even begging was to be allowed. They placed themselves completely in God's hands, confident that He would give them whatever was necessary. Their desire was to reform the secular clergy; for this they wanted their own house to be in order. And they carried their program through to a successful conclusion. It is important to remember that all this occurred in the year 1524, the first year of the pontificate of the politically oriented and pleasure loving Medici, Pope Clement VII (1523-1534). The papal curia was totally immersed in the benefice hunt: this was the world in which Carafa resigned both his bishoprics.

The year 1527 was a turning point for many of the humanists; the Confraternity of Divine Love spread from Rome throughout Italy. The Theatines came to Venice with Carafa and Gaetano. There they encountered a reform group whose most prominent member was the humanist Gaspar Contarini, a layman. They joined forces with him. It was in Venice that Carafa stated, in the form of a rule, the purpose of the order: the formation of blameless priests. This new order followed a policy of extreme caution in accepting new members, since their aim was to form an elite group within the Church.

Although the phenomenon of this small religious order joining forces with zealous reform circles is calculated to arouse our sympathy, it was certainly not adequate to the task of thorough renewal throughout the entire Church. In addition, the phenomenon was too isolated.

We now have to turn our attention to the papal court. It had been a fundamental law in the history of the Church, until the reign of Leo XIII, that badly needed reforms have not begun at the top but at the bottom, among groups that strove for renewal in the spirit of the following of Christ. This was the case with Cluny; it was true of St. Bernard in the twelfth century, of St. Francis and St. Dominic in the thirteenth, and it became eminently true in the sixteenth century. It is furthermore a fact that only if such a reform, started in the lower echelons, has been accepted and authoritatively promulgated by the supreme authority in the Church, can it become truly pervasive and effective. This, too, was the case in the sixteenth century.

In the stormiest years of the Reformation Pope Adrian

VI (1522-1523) was thoroughly committed to reform. To his awareness of the terrible conditions in the Church and his admission of the guilt of the Papal Curia we owe much of the improvement in the following decades. Adrian was one of those individuals whose sanctity goes unrecognized, who are not successful by worldly norms, but who play such a great and even decisive role in the Communion of Saints. But he had no time to put his plans into action, for he reigned for only twenty months. The times and even his own Curia opposed him. For these reasons the reform within the Church in the sixteenth century did not originate with the Papacy.

Passing over the reign of Clement VII, a frightfully vacillating Medici politician, we come in the fourth decade of the century to Paul III (1534-1549). Definitely a man of the Renaissance, he had come from the Rome of Alexander VI, and his career was closely bound up with the latter's vicious life. He was the father of a number of illegitimate children, whom he publicly acknowledged. His court was characterized by many of the unchristian, unedifying, and shocking practices which were common with his predecessor. Yet the most surprising aspect of his reign was that he was much more than a Renaissance pope: in fact his pontificate meant nothing less than the commitment of the Papal Curia to a program of reform within the Church.

Three facts are enough to prove this thesis: Paul III revitalized the College of Cardinals and made it into a religious and ecclesiastically oriented body; Paul III gave ecclesiastical approval to the Society of Jesus; and despite all the obstacles, he summoned a long overdue general council to meet in Trent.

The complexity of each of these phenomena, which had such a profound influence on the transformation of the

Church, precludes a thorough analysis of any of them. We must be satisfied with a few superficial observations, principally on the Council of Trent.

No event which profoundly reveals or affects the human spirit can be adequately described solely in terms of its material content. Equally important is the structure, entelechy, and function of any event within its own times and milieu and in terms of its subsequent development. The Council of Trent becomes an outstanding event both from the standpoint of the events of that time and their import on later ages.

One of the principal events, of course, was the doctrinal decree on justification, which Harnack felt could have halted the Reformation if it had come in time; the decree on Scripture and Tradition as sources of faith, on the sacraments, and especially on the Sacrifice of the Mass. Important too, for the transformation of ecclesiastical life, were the reform decrees of the third session (1562-3) on marriage, the training of the clergy, residence of the clergy, and the new breviary and missal which were published after the end of the Council. Though these decrees were a compromise which satisfied neither group in the Curia, and though in themselves the decrees were not a prime influence on the renewal of life in the Church (which was rather an effect of the new apostolic spirit of faith and prayer of which the Council itself was a product), still, because of the authority with which they were endowed, they did present a clear goal with an assured method of attaining it, and were a steadying and unifying influence of inestimable value.

The structure and tendency of the Council were of greater importance; in some respects these go beyond the reform decrees, but basically they simply incorporate these

decrees into an important line of development in the history
of the Church. This is an indication of the function of the
Council in terms of its own milieu and of later developments in the Church; through it we can get some indication
of its overwhelming historical importance.

The most important characteristic of Church history
in modern times, which distinguishes it from all earlier
periods, is the centrality of the notion of the Church itself.
To the beginning of our century, Church history developed
as the history of ecclesiastical centralization at Rome, in
order to secure ecclesiastical unity under the pope. From
this standpoint the Vatican Council is the great achievement and the true end-product of the whole modern age in
the Church. Trent made this development possible and
definitively inaugurated it.

The task was not easy for many obstacles had to be
overcome. The very summoning of the Council was not
without opposition; neither was it easy to satisfy canonical
formalities and secure political recognition on the part of
the European States. But in surmounting these difficulties
and in the task of translating its whole Christian and ecclesiastical world view into reality, it represented a victory for
the forces which wanted a Church strongly centered on the
Papacy, over those separatist tendencies which were moving in the direction of national Churches. At its very beginning, Trent fell under the shadow of the conciliar movement, which had once again shown signs of life at the very
beginning of the sixteenth century under Louis XII of
France, and now posed a real threat to the Papacy in the
form of a heretical German national council. Traces of
this same conciliar movement were apparent both during
and after Trent in various attempts at decentralization and
the setting up of national Churches. The danger was par-

ticularly grave in Spain first, then in France; later, during
the Enlightenment throughout Europe, it reached its climax
in the Bourbon courts and the apparently definitive victory
of Napoleon over the Papacy.

Naturally speaking, it is impossible to see how the unity
of the Church could have been preserved without Trent;
specifically, without the centralization of the Church
around the Holy See which Trent decreed and sanctioned.
The Council sprang in part from the justified struggle of
peripheral forces in the Church against the Papacy and the
corruption of the papal court, but through the Council the
Papacy triumphed over these peripheral democratizing elements and completely revamped its own image, through
this decisive step that prepared the way for the Vatican
Council.

Now we must say a few words about the revitalization
of the College of Cardinals under Paul III. The complete
secularization of the Papal Curia during the preceding
period was in large measure responsible for the Church's
problems. The Curia must bear the blame for the perversion of a primarily religious, medieval universalism into its
secular counterpart that developed in Avignon and was
completed in the Rome of the Renaissance. We know well
the words of Adrain VI about the den of iniquity which
was Rome and the harsh comment of St. Catherine of Siena
on the frightful vices of the papal court. To attempt a truly
Christian transformation within the papal court, was to
attack the true roots of the problem. Paul III did this in four
consistories (1535, 1536, 1540, 1542) where politics,
simony and nepotism had no part and men were elevated
to the cardinalate solely from Christian motives. It was at
this period that the able and influential layman Contarini
was elevated, and a number of others as learned and dedi-

cated as he, whose names constantly recur in the history of
the reform movement in the later decades of the sixteenth
century.

A number of these cardinals and other prelates, appointed to a commission by the Pope, at his request produced a document outlining plans for reform. In it and in
similar official documents it is quite easy to see the deep-
seated abuses in the Papal Curia and throughout Church
administration; but the documents also indicate a desire
to get at the truth and to effect a change. This latter was
something quite new. It was the spirit of Adrian VI, and it
proved that those whose task it was to guide the Church
were now taking their job seriously again. Luther had no
appreciation of this program of reform and consistently
made fun of it, but this attitude on his part was nothing
more than the practical denial of the first thesis on indulgences with which he began his revolt against the Church.
It is true that the spirit of this program was not the only
factor subsequently operative at the Papal Curia, but it
never ceased to influence the life and thought of the leading
ecclesiastical circles. Its spirit was fully developed in the
Council of Trent and put into action under the reforming
popes of the last half of the century.

Nevertheless, there was, of course, an element of ambiguity in the character of Paul III. Yet despite all of his defects from a Christian point of view, he must be credited
with one achievement of historic importance: the transformation of a worldly and politically orientated Renaissance
Papacy into an instrument of effective religious revival.

It is true that the forces striving for reform were still
not those of the Papacy, but were composed of clerics and
laymen quite far from Rome and the papal court. How

little the Papacy itself was involved in the reform movement and how little it could do to be of effective service
to the forces of revival, is clear from the two next pontifi-
cates. In the sixth decade of the century it was still possible
for one as morally disreputable as Julius III to reign, and
even the imposing figure of Paul IV, who as priest and
cardinal played a large part in getting the reform movement
started, was able to do little to further positively the movement, largely because of his predilection for the more grue-
some methods of the inquisition, his distrust of people, and
his short-sighted nepotism. (Negatively, his contribution
was greater and he did succeed in eliminating a number
of abuses.)

It is true that after the time of Paul III and following
a vast amount of effort by the most zealous reform groups
in the Church, the Papacy gradually assumed a central and
essential role in the reform movement, climaxed by the
election of Marcellus II to the Chair of Peter in 1555. The
succeeding pontiffs, Pius IV, Pius V, Gregory XIII, Sixtus
V, and Clement VIII, throughout the last forty years of the
sixteenth century show that the Papacy itself had undergone
a thorough inner revival and became capable of directing
the magnificent Catholic renascence which made such a
great impression both within and without the Church and
produced so many great saints. The work of these Counter-
Reformation popes was no longer primarily against Lutheranism which by this time had clearly become involved in
all sorts of internal doctrinal disputes and was already on
the way to a progressive dissolution. Calvinism had become
the new enemy and a much better organized and aggressive
foe. It was in the 1570's and 80's that the real danger of
the Reformation became apparent, as the doctrine of the
innovators seemed to be triumphing throughout France,

Poland, and Hungary. It seemed not unlikely that all of
Europe north of the Alps and the Pyrennees would be lost
to the Church.

If we are going to evaluate properly the achievements
of the reform movement within the Church, we must keep
in mind the violence of the attack leveled by the Protestant
Reformation against the Church over a wide front. The
Church's work of reform was carried on after decades of
rampant corruption from within, in an atmosphere of extreme crisis in which the Church had been thrown on the
defensive on all fronts. It is true that in this moment of
extreme danger the Church again manifested its most profound vitality internally and externally. In these decades
of reform and revival, the Church drew on inner resources
strong enough to check the threatened collapse, and build
the Church anew. In this we can and must see the hand of
Providence at work.

The Church was founded by Jesus Christ; its most characteristic mark, if we can speak of one characteristic mark,
is its holiness. Therefore, when we discuss the success of
the reform movement, our question centers on the holiness
of the Church as we discovered when we discussed the influence of the Confraternities of Divine Love, the Theatines, and the reform-minded Cardinals. The saints are the
ones who save the day, however. This is always the case
in the history of the Church; it certainly is true of the
sixteenth century. To a truly astounding degree, holiness
was manifested in the Church from the fourth decade of
that century onwards; the numbers, variety, and level of
heroism of the saints is simply amazing. We can give just
a few scanty indications.

The first example was the Jesuit Order, founded by
Saint Ignatius of Loyola (†1556). With his imposing syn-

thesis of zeal and discretion, his Order gave a vast number of confessors and martyrs to the Church in the sixteenth century. The achievements of this Order amounted to nothing less than the rescue of the Church at the time.

Next, the Capuchins who witnessed such a surprising period of development after a rather hesitant beginning. Their pastoral work among the ordinary people renewed the Church from its grass roots; this occurred after the Order itself underwent a renewal that brought them back to their ancient Franciscan ideals.

Again, the Reformed Order of Discalced Carmelites, with Saint Theresa of Avila and St. John of the Cross, each a miracle of prayer, penance, and organizational abilities. St. Theresa is particularly significant from our point of view since she concretized the reform movement in the Church, both from its inner wellsprings and as far as it was stimulated by the Protestant Reformation. Theresa felt a rending of the unity of faith in a personal way. She was deeply involved in the anguish of her age, although her striving for perfection, mystical prayer, penance, and the search for God have their roots in the life of the Church itself.

Other examples are innumerable: consider the attractiveness and originality of the Roman, St. Philip Neri (1515-1595). Consider, too, the many facets of the piety of St. Charles Borromeo and of the man whose election to the See of Peter he secured, St. Pius V, who put Trent's programs into action, and who had such devotion to the crucified Lord. Consider, too, the English and Irish martyrs and the heroic missionaries, especially, the towering figure of the great pioneer, St. Francis Xavier (†1552). These saints came from all segments of society; among them were men and women of all ages and of every conceivable type of personality. Many of them were men of prodigious vitality, gifted with great powers of organization in a truly creative sense. They tapped heretofore unsuspected resources in the Church and made masterful use of them.

Throughout these events, there began, both in the new orders and in the reformed ancient orders, in the papal court and its diplomatic apparatus, a complete transformation of ecclesiastical life that affected pastoral care, divine worship, and preaching; this manifested itself in the foundation and organization of missions in Asia, America and Africa, and in the organized care of the poor and the sick. We find a completely new concept of the Church's role in education which has become such an important factor in modern times.

Time and space unfortunately preclude detailed study of the infinitely varied ways in which the reform and revival flowered in the Church and the tireless and heroic work on the part of so many people which it involved. In fact, over and above the factors mentioned, we have the unparalleled development of what we might call secondary forces in the process of reform within the Church, that is, in literature, architecture, and sculpture. Think of what the great figure of Michelangelo alone means for the sixteenth century. His influence lasts until our own day, and it is the influence of a spiritual disciple of Savonarola and his preaching of reform and penance. Today, when the classical ideal has lost its appeal to many, there might be some objection to the earlier works of the master on the grounds that they overemphasize external form and smack of a pagan naturalism. These objections have their point, but they obviously cannot be dealt with here; certain of his works do show a predominant interest in formal anatomical structure; his subjectivity did have its dangers and would have to be analyzed against the background of his times and against the process

of his own inner development. But I think that I can justify
my position quite briefly. Some might feel that his *Pietà*
in St. Peter's is a little too smooth, too sleek. I would rec-
ommend to them that they examine it in detail, and suggest
that if they do, they will be struck by the majesty of the
dead Lord. The principal task, of course, which faces us
when we try to grasp the influence of Michelangelo as a
strictly religious factor, is that of resolving a great paradox: he was a Christian, deeply conscious of the world's
suffering and of original sin, who strove with all his energies for salvation; yet at the same time, he was so deeply
intoxicated with the recently discovered techniques of classic sculpture that the nude body was the only form in
which he felt able to express himself. The man who can
resolve this paradox will have some insight into the meaning of the master's slaves, who seem so reminiscent of the
old days of pagan antiquity, but are really the expression
of a profoundly insecure human being, striving with all his
might for salvation. Most noteworthy of all, his profoundly
religious outlook did not find expression completely apart
from the Church. This could well have happened if we
recall how strong-willed and headstrong he was, how conscious of his own powers and of his clashes with the popes
of his day. Yet he always remained a humble member of
this Church and his art proclaims it.

The study of history is of value only if we truly grasp
the meaning of the past, for then alone can our knowledge
of the past be put at the disposal of the present. The basic
laws of history have their lessons for us, not the symptoms.
We are interested not merely in the fact that a Catholic reform took place but much more in the laws of its structure
and development. Thus we must search for the inner law
that governed the activities of the great men we have men-

tioned. This inner law or principle was the mysterious
source of the Ignatian principle of obedience, the inner
freedom of Philip Neri, a friend of St. Ignatius, the mystic
ardor of Theresa of Avila, a much stronger character than
Bernini's statue would indicate, yet a figure of such profound humility in the midst of her great creative achievements. To find this inner law and analyze its workings
would be an attractive and rewarding study, but we simply
do not have time for this. Our concern must be more general; it is to determine whether behind the revival within
the Church any general laws of vital growth were operat-
ing.

Certain historical facts can be of assistance to us in this
study. The first is that no historically influential development comes about as a result of a complete break with the
immediate past. (Despite external appearances this is so
even in revolutions.) The second fact is that every important development in the history of the Church comes about
through a process of vital contact with the best contemporary forces. This is true also of the saint who changes
history; he never stands alone in his historical period, but
is deeply indebted to it.

The Saint does not leave the world so that he can watch
the world go by; he leaves it so that he can properly assess
it and then return and conquer it. If we accept these historical laws and apply them to the process of rebirth within
the Church in the sixteenth century, we discover two facts.
First the issues raised by the Reformation are consciously
or unconsciously accepted. It is not a question of simply
answering the objections of the reformers in an external
way, for when those objections are really grasped, they are
found to contain the Catholic answer, as is illustrated by
both the Council of Trent and the Jesuits. The central

questions concern grace, free will, and the visible Church; the solution or synthesis is the Catholic acceptance of both elements of the mystery and the Catholic assertion of the objective order of things. No matter how important the salvation of the individual soul, the guiding principle is: *Omnia ad majorem Dei gloriam.* God's honor is first and foremost. The second fact which we discover in these historical laws is quite astounding, considering our previous discussion of the problem of humanism. We find an affirmation of humanism; we encounter a genuine Christian humanism.

The possibility of a Christian humanism and its inner values and influence was the search for a solution that most profoundly characterized the ecclesiastical revival in the sixteenth century.

Whether we use the general term, "Christian humanism" or the more specific ones such as, "Christian culture," "Christian political science," or "Christian art," we are immediately faced with the problem of culture versus the Cross, the relation of culture with its overtones of pagan naturalism to the "new man," the baptized Christian who now lives in Christ. We are immediately aware of the tensions inherent in this situation; they can erupt with explosive force, for on these questions the entire culture of a Christian society, or more properly, a society composed of Christians, depends.

Back to the point: Christian humanism is the inner structural principle of Church reform. Note that this is not a problem for aesthetics; we are not interested in art or culture in themselves. We want to get to the heart of the matter and find out the relevance to Christian life and to the Church of artistic and cultural phenomena, particularly against the background of the religious revival of the

sixteenth century. And as we said, humanism as a value
was affirmed in that religious revival.

In view of our earlier remarks about humanism, this
probably strikes the reader as a surprising conclusion, since
we pointed out that the humanism of the times was a source
of real difficulty and extreme danger for the Church. We
said that it was not enough to enumerate the Christian elements which were still part of the humanism of the day,
but we would have to take into account what would have
happened if the specifically novel elements in that humanism had ever been fully realized. We found that humanism
was quite completely defined in the Renaissance Papacy,
which was noted not for the sanctification of the world but
for the secularization of the Church. And we pointed out
that Erasmus, by his indifference to dogma and his relativism, constituted a great danger to the Church. We are
still convinced of these earlier conclusions of ours.

But here, as always, reality is a complex area. We have
to realize that practically all of those whom we mentioned
in our sketch of Church reform in the sixteenth century
had received a humanistic training. The fact that there were
a number of theologians who were not humanists proves
merely that no single thesis can sum up the whole situation;
it does not disprove our assertion. We have the Confraternity of Divine Love and related confraternities, who quite
consciously put themselves under the protection of the
favorite Saint of the humanists, Jerome. We have Adrian
VI, Charles Borromeo and his Vatican Academy, Philip
Neri and his Oratory and its connections with the new
ideas in science and art, as exemplified by Palestrina. We
have Gregory XIII (1572-1585), the Jesuits with their
pedagogical methods and their doctrine of grace. We have
Sixtus V, the creator of the new Rome, Michelangelo, and

Vittoria Colonna, and finally, the leading lights of the
ecclesiastical revival in Spain and France toward the end
of the sixteenth century and throughout the seventeenth.

A number of questions can be asked about the humanistic achievements of these men. How much was of real
value in a Christian sense? What dangers of unchristian
values were present in moralism, for example, or the tendency to miss the rôle of the cross in the life of the Church.
The whole range of pressing and unsolved questions that
center on the concept of the *logos spermatikos,* a great and
genuinely Catholic concept, warn us to be prudent in our
judgment. We have to show much more reserve in these
questions in the Baroque period than in the period of a few
decades earlier that was absorbed in the first wave of newly
discovered Catholic values.

Regardless of individual cases, it remains true that the
leading figures of the ecclesiastical reform used the forms
of humanistic culture to expand, deepen, and purify the
Kingdom of God. As long as the spread of the Kingdom of
God is a sign of salvation, we can say that the blessing of
Christ was on their employment of humanistic culture.

Now that we have isolated Christian humanism as a
central structural principle of Church reform, we must
analyze something of its content. Here, despite appearances, things are quite simple. The age of mediocrity and
a merely negative correctness is over: "I came to bring fire
from heaven and my will is that it burn." The fire sent from
above did begin to burn and it burned more brightly than
ever, with the result that the ancient faith became new
again and strong enough to move the mountains of obstacles and abuses in its way. The mystical body of Christ once
more became a follower of the Cross, and the spirit of service and abnegation once more manifested themselves to a

heroic degree. This was the basis of the revival, an un-
merited, free gift. To a certain extent, when we encounter
it, our study of the motivating power of the Catholic revival
is at an end.

But grace is not magic. Its working is not external, but
follows the laws of nature, since these, too, are from God.
Then, as always, its workings are conditioned by the climate
of the times. Here we are surprised that when we examine, as
it were, the inner life of the Catholic reform, we come to the
same complex of problems expressed in the terms *humanism*
and *renaissance*. We have seen many times that Church
reform was nothing less than a rebirth; but humanism and
the Renaissance were brought about by those who sought
for a rebirth, whose cry was "back to the original sources."
This was the inspiration of both the pagan and Christian
Renaissance, and the triumph of the Christian Renaissance
was the reform within the Church of the sixteenth and seventeenth centuries. Note that it is not as though humanism had
two possible lines of development, Christian and pagan; it
remained true that the distinguishing characteristic of humanism was not its orientation toward God but toward man
and the world. In Christian humanism, humanism is not the
dominant element. But this does not alter the fact that the
enthusiasm and vitality of the idea of rebirth revitalized the
Church in a thoroughly creative way.

Whenever new and potentially significant ideas appear
on the historical scene, they are immediately subject to
widely differing interpretations. We find that in the secular-
ism of the Renaissance and in the abuses of the Papal
Curia, pagan tendencies won out. The cry, "back to antiquity," was understood as a call for beauty and pleasure.
In the reform movement within the Church on the other

hand, Christian factors were dominant and the cry was interpreted as a call for a return to the original purity of Christianity. The great enthusiasm of the Renaissance had joined forces with the profound desire for a Christian reformation.

We can fill in the outlines of this picture and grasp the richness of the reform movement within the Church by examining the Counter Reformation in the seventeenth century.

The concept of Counter Reformation is complex and somewhat ambiguous; if we distinguish it radically from the inner rejuvenation of the Church, we inevitably reduce it to something external and not too important, the reconquest of areas lost to the Church with the then current methods. These methods consisted to a great extent of external force, according to the pagan principle, *cujus regio, ejus religio*. It is true that the importance of this reconquest in the total process of Church history cannot be exaggerated, and we do not question its justification in the face of the forces on the side of the reformers that first precipitated the situation. But only an extremely positivistic view of Church history could be satisfied with reporting the fact that so much territory had been won back. Prescinding from the weakening of the foundations of religious conviction brought about by repeated changes of allegiance, the use of force itself often weakened the power of faith and charity. However, in many other cases, a return to the Church brought about by violent means did result in reintegration into the life of the Church. But the Catholic cannot shut his eyes to the tragedy involved and to the limitations of these methods. They bear all the earmarks of original sin. The Kingdom of God is spread through the contradiction in practice of the fundamental law of the Kingdom. God is love and the Lord made the law of love the beginning and end of His Kingdom.

However, Counter Reformation has a deeper meaning. In its best sense, it means a spiritual reconquest, that is nothing but the manifestation and result of the forces of reform and revival within the Church. A few examples will make this clear. For the first group of Jesuits Counter Reformation was nothing more or less than an immediate manifestation of an insatiable hunger for souls, the acceptance of the Lord's missionary injunction with the zeal for souls and cheerful self-dedication it implied. This was a fire that burned, that inspired, that first warmed and then enkindled others, and led them to extend unselfishly the Kingdom of Jesus Christ. Think of Peter Canisius (1521-1597) or Cardinal Stanislaus Hosius (†1579). In both there were political overtones, but these were employed as means in the religious struggle. Their whole story is that of a hunger and thirst for justice sake, and it would be ridiculous to regard their work as an example of one of the Church's power plays, or as indicative of "Roman intrigue," "Jesuit craftiness," or anything of the kind.

Think of the profound ardor of St. Theresa of Avila, who suffered so deeply at the separation of the reformed churches. In her mystic zeal to heal the split, she sent her spiritual forces across the Pyrenees.

The seventeenth century was, if anything, even more remarkable. During this period France was the political and cultural leader of Europe. More important from our point of view, it was an area where sanctity flowered. We know that both spiritually and politically there were weaknesses, but we want to grasp France's grand *siècle* as a unity, without doing violence to the factors under discus-

sion. It is likewise true that the upper levels of French
society were often morally corrupt, not particularly strong
in their faith, especially those who were most influenced by
the culture of the court during the period of French abso-
lutism. In the person of Cardinal Richelieu and his unscrup-
ulous policies the unchristian political mores of the sixteenth century and of Francis I lived on and constituted a
deadly threat to the Christian ideal. But Catholic unity in
France was assured in the person of Henry IV (1593-
1610) in a somewhat unchristian manner. But once this
Catholic unity was a fact, over and above national unity,
we find another culture that was not satisfied with mere
Christian correctness, but strove for real sanctity. European
culture flowered in France and nowhere more than in her
saints. This was the classic period of French literature.
Among its leading men are saints or at least men who lived
essentially from Christian motives.

Bishop Francis de Sales (†1622), the true pastor. He
was the saint who was so attached to his home, but led the
heroic religious revival of Chablais. He was the master of
individual pastoral care, the kindly founder of asceticism
for those in the world. He taught us the secret of striving
for holiness in the midst of all of the world's confusion.
He was the man of inner freedom and victorious optimism,
the inexhaustible preacher and confessor, a man of the
most refined tastes, but capable of deep sympathy with the
simple piety of ordinary folk, a priest of overwhelming
charity, of whom St. Vincent de Paul remarked: "O God,
how good you must be, if the Bishop of Geneva is as good
as he is." And above all, he burned with love of God and
lived entirely in dependence on the divine will.

Bishop Fénélon (†1715) with his *amour desintéressé*
is another great figure of this period, and an heroic exem-

plar of simple obedience to the Church. Bossuet (†1704) is forceful, complex, influential, one of the greatest preachers of all time. Blaise Pascal (†1662) is also worthy of mention. He was not only a scientific genius, but his high religious idealism presents a challenge which it is not easy to sidestep. He was an attractive and complex personality, endowed with a profound knowledge of God and of the ways to approach Him, but at the same time aware of the radical limitations of the human spirit in the face of the Infinite. The latter was reflected, on the personal level, in his consciousness of his sinfulness as a creature.

We have given but a few examples of the sanctity and mysticism that flowered during this period; many others are given in Henri Brémond's *Histoire du sentiment religieux en France*. We must at least mention the great preachers, Bourdaloue and Massillon. Over and above the saints and mystics themselves, think of the privileged souls who were directed by them, either directly or in letters that are now a priceless heritage.

Of course, some serious questions still have to be asked. Both before and after the Council of Trent the temptation to a comfortable mediocrity presented the same attraction as always to those who were striving for perfection. Remember, too, that although in the sphere of pastoral care and prayer the picture is good, in that of cultural life in general, in politics, and in the relationship of Church and State, the picture is not at all encouraging. In the first half of the seventeenth century alone, France was torn many times with bloody strife, by Richelieu's struggle against the Huguenots and the feudal nobility. In Spain, too, at the time literature and the arts were flowering, we note threatening signs of decline in both Church and State.

It would take a careful study to determine to what extent the ecclesiastical revival was due to a deepening of the life of faith and the consequent growth in sanctity or to the ambition and sense of power of the churchmen of the day. The latter is certainly apparent in the narrowly nationalistic policies pursued by most of the Catholic princes of the day. Still it was a complex age, from the Curia with its new dedication to pastoral care to the leading lights of the artistic and literary revival, who used their talents in the service of the Church. Yet even from the religious standpoint, Michelangelo's successors cannot approach the deadly seriousness of the "Last Judgment" in the Sistine Chapel or the embodiment of pure adoration represented by the cupola over St. Peter's.

These reservations, however, which we make in evaluating this period indicate its greatness, the creative tensions at work in its men of genius. Richelieu (†1642) cannot be summarily rejected; to do so would be superficial. He was the complete embodiment of the medieval union of Church and State, with distinctly modern, nationalistic overtones. A Catholic, priest, bishop and cardinal, he prayed and offered Mass and was careful to secure the regular attendance at Mass of the soldiers besieging La Rochelle. He thought nothing, however, of the cold-blooded sacrifice of the Catholic Faith in Germany, that meant nothing less than the disruption of the unity of the Catholic Faith in the West. And he did this in the name of French nationalism. It is true that this was a perversion of his vocation as a Christian and a priest, but it is difficult to condemn him without at the same time condemning the same type of policy at Rome, whether in acute form in Alexander VI's treaty with the Turks or the subsequent papal policy which saved the Reformation, or in more moderate form in certain of its manifestations throughout the entire *ancien régime* since the end of the sixteenth century.

It is even more difficult to make a judgment in the case of the tireless preacher and strict Capuchin, Père Joseph LeClerc, the gray eminence—Richelieu's close collaborator and a man of rare political gifts.

With all these reservations, this was a period in France outstanding for its sanctity, a good example of the fruit of the inner reform of the Church in the sixteenth century. The picture of thorough ecclesiastical revival which it presents is attractive.

In our abbreviated study of this period, we cannot bypass Spain. We noted in dealing with the question of the origins of ecclesiastical reform that much more historical work needs to be done before it will be possible to appraise the relative importance of Spain and Italy in that period. This is also true in the case of the seventeenth century. But there is no doubt that Spain's contribution during both periods was of decisive importance. In the seventeenth century, Spanish achievements in art and literature were recognized throughout the world, as profound expressions of the Catholic religious ideal. After the literary productions of St. Theresa and St. John of the Cross in the sixteenth century came the many works of the two priests, Lope de Vega (1562-1635) and Calderon (1600-1681). (Unfortunate examples, perhaps, from the standpoint of their personal lives, for these were characterized by benefice hunting and low moral standards.) This too was the period of the great Cervantes (1547-1616), a member of a Third Order.

Finally, we cannot forget the tremendous influence that this predominantly Romance Catholic culture had on the northern lands, even those which were by now Protestant.

With the exception of Molière and Shakespeare (perhaps not an exception) all of the leading literary lights were Catholic.

In Germany we find a completely different picture. Even if, with Wilhelm Oehl and Günther Müller, we take as sympathetic a view as possible of seventeenth-century German Catholic culture, for the first half of the century its poverty in comparison with the Latin lands is shocking. The only bright lights in the gloom are the new developments in music, in learning (with the Salzburg Benedictines, for example) and, after the middle of the century, the development of Baroque architecture. (The question of the religious value of the latter is too complicated to discuss here.)

There were a number of Catholics in seventeenth-century Germany whose religious influence is still operative today. Among them are Abraham a Santa Clara (†1709), Procopius von Templin (†1680) and especially Martin von Kochem (†1712), Friedrich von Spee (†1635), and Angelus Silesius (†1677) with his spiritual lyrics. We also have Jacob Balde (†1688) who wrote in Latin and who was famous throughout Europe, whom Herder called "Germany's poet for all times." For their achievements Germany can be grateful.

No critically honest judgment can fail to admit how inferior Germany was to the Romance lands in the quantity and quality of their writings. Of course the explanation is apparent: Germany was bled white in the religious wars, and the Reformation left Catholic Germany in a state of exhaustion. The hopelessness of the situation is found in the picture drawn by St. Peter Canisius in the 1560's that suggests the very nadir of decline. In the 1570's some of the programs of reform would seem to indicate that not even a beginning had been made. There was a shortage of priests and many of these were not good enough. From the situation in Germany it is easy to see how much the Council of Trent was still just a promise of things to come.

We are concerned primarily with the religious vitality of the Catholic renewal. From this standpoint in the sixteenth and seventeenth century Germany must be reckoned as nought and, hence, a detriment to the whole Church. But the great revival in southern Europe remained a fact. It seemed almost a miracle: the very life of the Church seemed to have been poisoned, but it produced its own antidote and proceeded to rejuvenate itself. The Reformation forced on the Church a struggle, the likes of which had never been seen, and the Reformation itself moved forward on the crest of a Christian revival. The Gospel of faith alone was preached with great power and zeal. Finally, in the 1560's and 70's it seemed as though the Reformation in its now Calvinist form would sweep the Church away. What many in the Church had been solemnly prophesying for centuries seemed to be an accomplished fact. A number of good Catholics, who believed firmly in the indestructibility of the Church, could not help thinking that it was living in a state of suspended animation.

Finally, when, as Harnack put it, the Evangelical Churches, including the Calvinist, had exhausted their religious vitality, the Catholic Church was still standing with renewed vitality. The Church had survived onslaughts unparalleled in her history; a whole world had collapsed around her; she had been declared dead; somehow, inconceivably, she had rejuvenated herself and stood surrounded by her works to prove it.

It is possible to grasp what marvels this meant only if we have seen how sick the Church was and only if we admit that collapse seemed imminent. This is a case where strict honesty is rewarded, because then the Church's inner revival in the sixteenth century will be viewed as a most impressive historical proof of the divinely-given indestructibility of the Church.

We must never forget that history is more than a summary of the events of the past. The process of history is always incomplete and is continuous with the events of our own day. In this sense, history is something for us to achieve. This is certainly true of that which we have made the theme of this chapter, for the Catholic revival of the sixteenth and seventeenth century was never finally brought to completion.

Taking the Pontificate of Gregory XIII as the high tide of this revival, from the Curia downwards there were notable defects from the strictly religious viewpoint. There was an element of moralism in the revival. Where the Catholic reform met the Reformation head on, it was frequently characterized by negative polemics and a defensive attitude—a kind of secondhand substitute for the positive religious ideal. Even the specifically Catholic achievements of the period have their share of ambiguity and contradiction. Theological solutions and policies of Church government were frequently quite narrow and inspired only by the spirit of the Counter Reformation. We know what a damaging influence this inheritance has exercised on the Church's activity and her effectiveness even in recent times. Think, too, of the religious poverty of the Christian art of the Baroque period and the full significance of the rapid progress of the Enlightenment in France. P. Hasard summed it up well, saying that until 1680 all Frenchmen thought like Bossuet; from 1720 on they thought like Voltaire.

It is true that in the history of the Church there are no periods without defects and weaknesses. This is a conclusion both of practical historical experience as well as of our Lord's statement in the Gospel. It would be particularly naïve to look for an almost-perfect period so soon after the period of almost indescribable decay which we have seen, especially since many of the factors which favored the decay continued right through the sixteenth and seventeenth century up to the time of the French Revolution.

And so, while the ecclesiastical revival of the sixteenth and seventeenth century is a source of real joy and grateful pride to Catholics, at the same time it has an implied warning and poses a real obligation: Reform within the Church is not a task of merely the eleventh, thirteenth or sixteenth century; reform within the Church is a permanent theme in Church history. This is the *metanoia* on which the Gospel puts so much emphasis.

This brings us back to the central point of our discussions. We see once more that the original concerns of both the Catholic reform and the Reformation were the same. Luther, who originally wanted reform in the one Church, expressed this profoundly Catholic concern in one of his first public utterances as the crisis of the sixteenth century arose: "When Our Lord Jesus Christ said, 'Do penance,' He wanted the whole life of the Christian to be a penance." This call for penance strikes at the roots of externalism and superficiality. It is something genuine. It is more than an interest in *metanoia*. It calls for something hard and difficult. Penance, ultimately, calls for Christian existence in faith and prayer. And nothing other than this is needed today.

Originally Luther wanted this renewal in the one

Church; let us accept his challenge and submit to Our Lord's great desire: *ut omnes unum sint!* This is the concern which has brought us together and which has been the object of our prayers.

We have to be willing to learn the lessons that history has to teach us; our evaluation of the Church reform in the sixteenth century can, in all probability, be of use to us as we face our task today. The story of Church reform then was a story of modest beginnings in small circles, of individuals who took their tasks seriously, of reverence for the great mystery involved in the process of growth, of doing what had to be done without any petty disputes about the way to do it, without looking for immediate results or personal gain. It was a story of facing up to the real problems of the day simply and humbly, and of approaching them with a spirit of truth, of love and of sacrifice. All spiritual, moral, and religious growth is governed by that primordial law of Christianity: lose your life in order to gain it. The seed must first die in order to bring forth fruit.

IV

The Basic Concerns
of the Reformation and
Catholicism Today

The structure of the Reformation is very complex. To speak of its basic concerns would be an oversimplification and we use the term merely to point up the main concerns shared by the leading reformers. Luther himself is the foremost of these, because the Reformation can be traced to him and because to our own day he has remained the most significant religious influence in the reformed Churches. He is to some extent regarded as a common authority among them.

Following the introduction, this lecture will be divided into three parts: (A) Areas where the Catholic Church agrees with the concerns of the reformers; (B) Areas where the Catholic Church is in disagreement or limited agreement with the concerns of the reformers; (C) Catholicism today in relation to those concerns.

Our historical study of the causes of the reformation has shown us: (1) The Reformation is a Catholic concern not only in the sense that the Church is in opposition to it, but that Catholicism shares the guilt and responsibility for it. Adrian VI gave this point genuine Christian expression. (2) The Reformation is also a Catholic concern insofar as it was partly responsible for reform within the Church. (3) Finally, the destiny of all mankind has been profoundly affected by the Reformation. There is no area of human life, whether it be religion, politics, culture, science or economics, that would not be essentially different if it were not for the fact of the Reformation. In many important respects this is true of the Catholic Church. (4) The Reformation has essentially and inescapably changed the conditions of Christian existence for more Christians than existed before the Reformation. This is an extremely significant fact which has simply not been taken into account.

With a consideration of these facts, if we try to look at the Reformation in a deeply Christian way, we can say this: If great historical events have a meaning, and if the Christian concept of divine providence, in which nothing takes place apart from God's will, is to have meaning, and if history is truly God's handiwork, then the great cataclysm that was the Reformation must have a significant rôle in the divine plan of salvation and hence present a real challenge to humanity, to Christendom, and to the Church of Christ.

When we talk about the basic principles of the Reformation, we are talking about its religious concerns. These are of prime importance and other interpretations mistake peripheral considerations for the central one, no matter how important the former may be. By religious concerns we mean primarily the dogmatic teaching of the Reformation. This leads to the question whether it is permissible to equate the Reformation with the new doctrines that became current in the sixteenth century, or is the Reformation to be understood in strictly formal terms. Was Luther's revolt against ecclesiastical authority merely a beginning, to be prolonged and continued as it gradually reveals its inner meaning and thus calls continually for new interpretation? Was Luther's preaching merely a question that demands an answer through the centuries and in our own day? In other words, did Luther's interpretation of Scripture have a merely passing value, one that was conditioned by the period, or did it claim to have the only meaning of revelation, binding on all men at all times. If the latter is true, with what right? To answer this question we will turn to Luther himself and to the New Testament.

Luther was first and foremost a preacher of the Gospel of Jesus Christ. Now what value does Luther himself attribute to his interpretation of the Gospel? Does he think that there is room for any other interpretation than his own? To answer the question properly in all details would demand a lengthy article, but without that a definitive answer can be given.

In answering the question let us think first of all of Luther's intellectual formation which we studied in the second lecture. We know that it was extraordinarily exclusive and that he himself was extremely intolerant. He made his views quite clear in the matter we have under discussion here. Christianity in its complete form has been given us once and for all in revelation; so true is this that there can be no development properly speaking. Christianity is a doctrine susceptible of only one interpretation, which, Luther affirmed, he had rediscovered, and his interpretation was to be binding for all times. Whatever contradicts his interpretation owes its origins to the Antichrist and the powers of hell. Luther left no doubt that this was his opinion, whether his opponent of the moment was the Pope, Zwingli and the Anabaptists or whether he was lamenting the doctrinal disputes that were to come after him. Remember that Luther challenged one and all to test his doctrine by the Gospel, and in all of these discussions there is not a single example of his yielding a dogmatic point or changing his interpretation. In his preaching, he was a proponent of the most absolute dogmatic intolerance.

As a result we can see that to define Luther and the Reformation in any but dogmatic terms, that is, in a purely formal manner, would certainly contradict Luther's own understanding of the movement. But here we must face a familiar objection: it is said that Luther himself did not see or even suspect the ultimate meaning of his teaching and his action. The real meaning of the Reformation simply could not be grasped by anyone of that day.

This is an important objection. It touches on the ultimate meaning of history as it runs its course in a world infected with original sin. We see that once human words and actions have entered the stream of history, the very men who originated them have little control over them. They follow their own laws and, at the most critical junctures, seem to escape direction entirely.

It is true that the Reformation in itself and in its development has its own proper historical meaning which we can determine no more completely than we can that of the meaning of history itself in the divine plan for the universe. For, in fact, some developments of the Reformation shook Western Civilization to its foundations. We will speak of them later.

But these developments which were really contradictions of the Reformation cannot in any sense be thought of as a fulfillment of its ideals, as further developments or even as insignificant changes. They are nothing less than a reversal, a denial, and the destruction of the essential nature of the Reformation. This remains true although we recall briefly that certain fundamental doctrines of the Reformation, such as salvation by faith alone, and the separation of the believing subject from the objective grounds of his faith, are responsible for the intellectual and psychological characteristics of modern man. The thesis that insists the Reformation is to be interpreted strictly and formally is a logical consequence of a radically positivistic and therefore materialistic conception of history.

The New Testament provides proof of the same kind, insofar as Luther is in agreement with the New Testament. Christianity is not merely brotherly love or walking in the light; it is the proclamation of a doctrine which is true and the rejection of a doctrine which is false. The Gospel is not abstract and theoretical doctrine; it is life and power. But it is still a true doctrine which can be recognized and adequately described. In the New Testament and in the early Church, good will was not the only criterion; the affirmation or denial of an objectively knowable truth counted also. This truth, given and revealed by God, was recognizable to such a degree that Paul had no hesitation in condemning to hell an angel who would preach a gospel other than that which he himself has been preaching.

In summary, we can say that Luther and the Reformation understood themselves in terms of dogma. By the fact that they did so, they were in formal agreement with the New Testament. Therefore we must understand Luther and the reformation in dogmatic terms.

A final preliminary question merits our attention: Should we adopt opposite positions as a point of departure?

This is certainly a possibility. At one time absolute denial at any cost certainly had its part to play. Thus, at the very beginning of the Reformation, Eck and Cochläus used this method to shake unsuspecting Catholics out of their lethargy to make them realize that this was no question here of reform within the old Church, but of something new and irreconcilably hostile to the Church. (I think it is obvious that we are making no attempt to justify the patent shortcomings of the polemics of that day.)

But this approach is inadequate; for one thing, we are not interested today in a categorical denial of each and every principle of Luther's. What we are seeking is understanding and a profound inner confrontation of views. Our awareness of the deficiencies in human and Christian terms that sparked the Reformation has prepared us for this. Yet the principal difficulty is that, if we start from opposite positions, we make it impossible to understand the scope and the significance of the new doctrine.

Furthermore, we must distinguish between the primitive religious concerns of Luther and the Reformation and the theological conclusions that were developed from them. This distinction is not merely a useful one to help us find the core of Luther's doctrine in areas in which he hesitated; it is an absolute necessity. For not only were completed and fully structured theological theses adduced to justify the break with the old Church, but also the more basic religious concerns responsible for them. These primitive religious concerns continued to play a decisive rôle in Luther's case, both in determining what he rejected and what he was to add.

Luther's denial of the sacramental priesthood provides a good example. If we simply oppose the Catholic doctrine to Luther's, we have, it is true, correctly expressed an objective state of affairs, but this doesn't help us to see the problem and to understand how Luther came to his denial. God knows that the denial of the sacramental priesthood is an important concern of Luther and the Reformation, but it is not a primitive concern; it is a consequence arising from a much deeper level. Luther rejected the sacramental priesthood because he saw in it a negation of what he conceived to be a prime concern of the Gospel. He saw it as an encroachment on his doctrine of justification by faith alone. Here we see another aspect: whatever reservations we may have to make in regard to the "faith alone" doctrine, here at least the Catholic doctrine and that of the Reformation are one and the same.

This brings up a question of great importance for our whole discussion: Is it possible that theological considerations and conclusions have widened the gap unnecessarily? Was the Reformation to its own and our detriment conceived in too theological a fashion? Did it become more theological than was appropriate to its fundamental religious concerns?

We turn now to the first part of our more general question: the concerns of the Reformation and of the Evangelical Churches with which Catholics are in agreement. Let us begin by enumerating some of the prime religious concerns of the Reformation.

One central concern was enunciated by Luther in 1517 in his first thesis on indulgences: "When Our Lord Jesus Christ said, 'Do penance,' He wanted the whole life of the Christian to be a penance." This thesis demands that the Christian take the matter of salvation seriously for his whole life, and declares war on everything mechanical in the sphere of religion, particularly in the reception of the sacraments. It puts the emphasis on a righteousness that is interior and demands personal piety. This first public proclamation of the reformer remained a central concern during his whole life.

In opposition to clericalism and the evils for which the Curia was responsible, Luther preached the universal priesthood of all Christians and the freedom of the Christian.

In place of the rational method of scholasticism, as exemplified in its formal definition of faith, the framing of concepts of God and justification, in fact, in its whole description of the process of salvation, Luther strongly emphasized that aspect of revelation not accessible to reason. He demanded a faith that embraced the Father in trust—a Father, by the way, much more vital than the kindly and forgiving Father of an oversentimentalized prayer.

The whole course of Luther's spiritual development inclined him to see man primarily as a sinner; consequently, he teaches that man is and remains a sinner.

Luther believed passionately that the riches of Holy Scripture are inexhaustible; the Word of Scripture has an unconditioned primacy over the theology derived from it. Luther proposed the concrete religious and prophetic message of the Bible in its fullness and on its own terms and thus had no desire to see it transposed into a rational theological system.

These are merely some of the concerns of the Reformation. We have intentionally given them but partial formulation; yet even in this fragmentary form, they are not just subsidiary concerns but central demands of the reformers. Let us begin by examining these concerns in the positive form in which we have presented them, prescinding initially from the more proximate determinations and additions with which they may be to some degree essentially bound up in the tradition of reform theology. Every Catholic is in full agreement with them. For without a doubt what Luther is asking for is a serious Christian commitment to Christianity. He is seeking a Christianity that is deeper, more interior, more spiritual, simpler, and more authentic. He sees the danger of finding a natural substitute for revealed Christianity. He leans to the terms used in the Bible and the liturgy to speak of the Christian message. Here we have transcended the polemical and are face to face with a positive

Christian ideal. Luther is speaking here with a Catholic voice, a voice which reveals the Catholic heritage which was and remained so much a part of Luther, and a voice which we unfortunately, though understandably enough, failed to hear for so long a period after his attack and after he left the Church.

Note well that when we say "Catholic" here, we do not mean merely according to the criteria of the Council of Trent. We mean "Catholic" according to criteria always accepted in the Roman Church, as they were expressed in the official *lex orandi,* for example, the Missal, and were officially recognized and realized even in Luther's time. I would summarize these considerations in the following form: There are basic concerns of the Reformation with which Catholics are in full agreement. They are affirmed on the Catholic side precisely because they manifest essential postulates of the Christian revelation.

This surprisingly profound Catholic affirmation of concerns of the Evangelical and Reformed Churches is of significantly wider scope, as is apparent by looking at a number of individual concerns of the reformation. We will simply enumerate a few of them:

1. Man and his world are as nothing before God.

2. No one is justified without God and even the justified man remains an "unprofitable servant." (This consciousness of being a sinner before God is clearly affirmed in the Catholic liturgy, where the Church addresses us as sinners right up to the time of communion. It is always one of the basic convictions of the saints and a basic principle of the theology of St. Thomas Aquinas, the Common Doctor.)

3. Without faith there is no Christian life and all justification comes from faith.

4. God's grace is absolutely indispensable not only for

the beginning of Christian existence but also for its con-
tinuance and development. Even the justified man needs
grace for any action that is availing to salvation.

5. God's grace is always a free gift.

6. God is our Father; we approach Him through a
trusting gift of ourselves to Him through His Son. What is
needed is love, not a servile fear based on law; before all
else, Christianity is the proclamation of the good news of
salvation.

7. The freedom of the Christian is an essential characteristic of the man who has been saved.

8. The God who freely gives Himself is also the God
who is our judge and who makes stern demands.

9. In preaching and in theology, the Lord Jesus, the
Person of the Lord, is to have absolute primacy.

10. Not only does the word of God have a truth content, but it is endowed with the power to save. The liturgy
expresses this same idea in the prayer said by the priest
after the Gospel; "May our sins be blotted out through the
words of this Gospel."

We need no exhaustive and complicated proof; it is
sufficient merely to list these truths to show that they are
the common property of both Catholics and the original
Lutheran reform. This is an important affirmation, for it is
necessary that many Evangelical Christians who think that
these doctrines are specifically "Reformation" doctrines
come to realize that they are really Catholic doctrines. Despite all of the areas that still divide us, it is most significant
that Evangelical Christians are coming to make this affirmation in ever-increasing numbers.

Luther was deeply estranged from the Rome of his day
which he saw as worldly and essentially foreign, but he
was in vital contact with all the forces operative in German

popular piety and in the awakening sense of German nationality. As a result, he demanded for Germans a prayer in the German language in the official liturgy, though he was far less radical than Zwingli in this regard.

Germany was the land where the Reformation began, and this concern of Luther's demands a little more discussion. It fronts on the larger question of the relation between Christianity and the German character and of the propriety of the influence of specifically Germanic forms on Christian existence in Germany, and further on the question of the relation of the nation and the Catholic in general.

If we want to get an objective and historically correct view of this problem, it is necessary not to confuse the sixteenth century with the twentieth. Neither Luther nor the Reformation attached as much importance as we do to national or popular spirit, even prescinding from the more frightful aberrations of nationalism in our times. This is true also for the religious question, our primary concern. It concerns the liturgy in the German language.* Catholicism is in a position to offer a solution to this problem, because on Catholic principles there is no obstacle to using the vernacular in the liturgy. For the Catholic Church is not really international, but supranational. She does not strive to replace national culture or reject its value, but presupposes it as grace presupposes nature. Furthermore, a strictly theological estimate of the relevance of national elements within Christianity is based on the recognition of man's natural capacity to cooperate in the process of salvation, which is, of course, an explicit Catholic position. Finally, the history of the Catholic Church and the Church as a

* No attempt has been made to revise the author's views to conform to the liturgical renewal instituted by the Second Vatican Council —Editor's note.

contemporary phenomenon cannot be understood unless we realize that within the Church there is and always has been a Catholic concept of a Church with the different characteristics of the various nations of its members. We must not forget that the official proclamation of the Church's message was quite naturally in the language of those to whom it was directed, not limited to the official language of the Roman world.

If we are going to understand the situation, it is important to disabuse ourselves of the notion that a Church with specifically national characteristics is also a Church without ties to Rome. The consciousness of the unity of the Church is so much a part of its heritage from the earliest times that even the lack of communication with Rome did not disturb this unity. Of course, even the tension that exists between a "national" church and the universal Roman Church cannot be equated with contradiction in the area of dogma. The very word *Catholic* implies a rejection of leveling influences and an acceptance of the natural tensions.

With these presuppositions we can see that the whole period of the early Middle Ages is proof of our thesis to such an extent that the pre-eminently universal Church of the Middle Ages could not have come about unless the way had been prepared by the predominantly national Church structure of the preceding period. This is true of the period of strikingly episodic character when the foundations of the Middle Ages were being laid up to and including the Carolingian Empire, which transcended national boundaries, and again after the collapse in the ninth century when the Church came under the domination of the Empire of the Ottos. The following centuries manifested all the degrees in which the national-church idea can be found within Roman Catholic unity.

A convincing proof is offered too in the period of the late Middle Ages when the national churches in the proper sense become dominant, either in the great monarchies of the West or in the German territories. With the sometimes fortunate, sometimes tragic, cooperation of the Papacy, the national churches form an essential part of the Church history of this period.

The Reformation period and the following centuries complete the illustration. We have to be on our guard and avoid any pseudo-apologetic mannerisms which would lead us to concentrate solely on tensions due to reactions to the papal curia. In writing the history of the Counter Reformation it has become very popular to concentrate on the political power of the Catholic countries. But for our part, we would like to emphasize that it was precisely the century of classical Gallicanism that was a century of saints. We discussed this phenomenon in our earlier third chapter.

We should not forget that today we have the Greek, Coptic, Armenian and Slavonic liturgies in a unity of the Roman Catholic with the Pope. So much for the principles involved.

As far as putting these principles into action, not much has been accomplished among the people of the West. This is especially true of the Germans, for they are completely deprived of the access that the Romance speaking peoples enjoy with Latin in the Church. Here we are faced with a great task: To determine the relationship of the ideals of the Reformation with those of the Catholic Church for the mutual understanding of Catholics and Evangelical Christians. It is of supreme importance that Catholics recognize that there is question of a genuine and profound problem facing the Church, not just a practical move that might seem desirable to some. For myself, I can see only one answer to this question. For while gestures and actions have a universal symbolism, the individual word must be taken on its own terms and understood on its own terms if it is to accomplish its end and purpose. Thus, if the priest silently reads the Gospel at the altar, in a certain sense this action still plays a part in the sacrifice of the Mass, but it is very deficient from the standpoint of the prayer that the priest says just before reading the Gospel, when he asks to be cleansed and prepared for the proclamation of the Gospel which is to follow.

The Church was justified for centuries in keeping a tight rein on this area, because it was above all necessary to safeguard the unity of the Church against separatist tendencies. We must remember that from the fifteenth century on, the vernacular movement was a characteristic of heretical and separatist movements. In our day, however, the unity of the Church is not threatened and no Catholic separatist movement would have a chance. Thus it is significant and quite proper that the vernacular question should come up again; for the same reason, we have to realize that it is an authentic and profound existential problem. It is not a question whose scope can be adequately delimited and an attempt to provide a complete program of solution would be a rationalistic form of interference in what should be a process of growth. But the justification for an intelligible liturgy cannot be questioned. Although the demand for the same should be satisfied gradually and with caution, it would be extremely unfortunate if it were not to be satisfied at all. For if such a profound and justifiable desire fails to find legitimate recognition, it will force its own solution, even an illegitimate one. The spread of the Reformation itself can serve as a warning here, because if it is possible to find one common denominator in this whole complex process, it could be said that the Reformation succeeded in Germany because in those times the Church in Germany was not sufficiently German.

Precisely because this question touches the very heart of the life of the Church, those who are most interested in genuine unity must be the first to realize that this work demands a holy prudence and a true sense of responsibility. Nothing could be more damaging to the satisfaction of this authentic human demand than an uncritical acceptance of opinions and feelings on the problem and its solution from every quarter. In matters, such as these, the most important point is not to set out a detailed program; it is much better to lay firm foundations and to form correct basic attitudes that give a free rein to growth. We need not fear: once the process of reform in this area is approved, what must be done will be done in good time.

In our own day we can see some signs of development in this sphere and a lessening of opposition to the vernacular in worship. Benedict XV emphasized during the First World War that the Church is not Latin, nor Greek, nor Slavic, but Catholic. Furthermore, the liturgical movement has made great progress in Germany and France. We should also note the privileges given, after the first World War to the Croatians, and in the mission areas of Japan, Manchuria, and China. What can happen in these areas cannot be absolutely impossible in France and Germany which at present certainly occupy a more important position in the Church. We have more evidence for this conclusion in the Papal Decree of Christmas Eve, 1943, which explicitly approved the practice, quite common in Germany, of using German prayers and hymns to enable the people to participate more closely in the Mass. It may well be that in the missions, particularly under the impetus of African nationalism, pastoral needs will make short work of obstacles which today seem to be so important. The translation of the Psalter, approved by Pope Pius XII in 1945, is quite significant in this regard, too, because it indicates the deep concern of the highest authority in the Church to make the content of revelation in its exact meaning available to the individual priest and religious.

This concern for the vernacular in official worship is another of those basic concerns of the Reformation to which there are no essential obstacles in the Catholic Church.

At the end of this part of our study, we can say that there is considerable agreement, on essentials, between a number of basic Catholic and Protestant concerns. We want to appreciate the full extent of this agreement, and let this appreciation have its effect on us. Differences which separate us are real, but we must go beyond them. This is not merely a question of policy, tact, or tactics; it is an attitude demanded by the facts as they stand, and one which rests on firm foundations. This becomes much clearer when we ask ourselves whether there would have been a Reformation in the sixteenth century if not only Luther and his coreligionists, but all men of the time had been fully and accurately aware that the doctrines we have mentioned are articles of the Catholic faith. Remember that even in the fragmentary form in which I have presented the concerns of the Reformation, Luther and others affirmed on innumerable occasions that they were either unknown to or rejected by the Catholic Church.

I have often asked this question of myself and in discussions with laymen and theologians of the Evangelical Church. Sometimes the answer was a firm *No!* At other times we felt that the break would by no means have certainly come about. In either case, I think the answer lends impressive support to my thesis. Another help to a solution would be to take my presentation of the Lutheran Reformation and, for the theological concerns enumerated, to substitute the Catholic theses I have mentioned above. As I have said before, if we do this it is impossible to see how the emotional conflict within Luther could have reached the state necessary to trigger his religious revolt.

We now turn our attention as fully and honestly to those issues of the Reformation in which Catholics can give but limited assent.

The limits of agreement are so striking that they seem to all but eliminate any close agreement we have just discussed. On important points the doctrine of the reformers is a denial and a rejection of articles of the Catholic faith, and the solemn condemnation of the doctrines of the reformers is the blunt expression of this fact.

Thus the Catholic affirms that in addition to the inviolable word of God, dogmatic tradition is also binding; that in addition to the universal priesthood and the obligations imposed by the individual conscience, there is also the specifically different sacramental priesthood and the infallibility of the Pope; that in addition to seeing man as a sinner, we must also see the good in man, the grace which is given to man to transform himself and to render his actions meritorious. There is no need to analyze each of these antitheses, but we should note that the revolt from the Church in the sixteenth century, with its restricted and one-sided affirmations, did not spring entirely from deep-seated theological convictions. To a great extent, accidental considerations that had nothing to do with religion played a great part in inducing civil authorities to embrace the new religion and introduce it into their territories. As we have seen, basic theological positions were influenced to a profound degree by polemic distortions, foolish exaggerations, and, often enough, simply the desire to reject the former Church and everything it stood for. It is of great importance, not only psychologically, but from the standpoint of objective truth, that both parties to the ecumenical dialog are becoming more and more aware of the fact that their real differences were exaggerated beyond all measure through hatred and short-sightedness in the heat of battle and that it is precisely elements which have nothing to do with doctrine that divided and continue to divide us.

Be that as it may, differences are there. They are serious and have had four hundred years to harden. Two different worlds confront one another and we must begin by trying to see them as they are in all their contrast.

But not all of these differences are, as is often affirmed, incapable of resolution. Even from an authentically Lutheran view some understanding of the Catholic position can be reached—a position which, in itself, contradicts the explicit formulation of Lutheran doctrine. For example, the affirmation of a sacramental priesthood is closely bound up with the meaning of the sacraments in general. In some respects the Reformation restricted the Catholic notion of sacrament, but in other respects it accepted the Catholic notion. In the Lutheran concept of the Lord's Supper and infant Baptism, the objective sanctifying power of the sacrament is clearly affirmed. It is true that within Lutheranism, these sacramental tendencies can be threatened, as is evident in the era of liberal theology, a period more or less of the past. While sectors of man's religious life which involve the notion of sacramentality, of worship in the true sense, and of the priesthood were neglected, the faith of the reformers was reduced more and more to a religion of the word. Quite necessarily, the gaps in man's religious consciousness were filled in with elements that had nothing to do with religion, or were pseudoreligious with no relation to revelation.

At present sacramental tendencies are much stronger among Lutherans. An article recently published by Sommerlath concerning Luther's doctrine of the Lord's Supper, if we prescind from certain obvious misunderstandings, approximates so closely the Catholic doctrine of *opus operatum* that the similarity is immediately obvious. Even the rejection of specific Catholic positions on the sacraments by present-day Lutheran theologians frequently shows more understanding of Catholic sacramental positions than was shown in all previous evangelical theology.

From this we can conclude that the more vital the concept and the reality of the sacrament as such become in the Evangelical Church, the easier it will be for them to understand Catholic concern for the sacramental priesthood. This presupposes, of course, that the sacrament is seen as it truly is in itself, in its proper form, which has nothing to do with the divinization of the human. A presupposition of mutual understanding in regard to this article of faith is a proper grasp of the Catholic notion of sacrament. Surprisingly enough, this understanding can be presented to Evangelical Christians with relative ease through an interpretation of Holy Mass, precisely the area where Luther chose to make his attack on the sacramental doctrine of the Church.

Luther attacked the Mass because he understood it as a purely human action and hence an idolatry. It is not difficult, however, to prove that his concept rested on assumptions that were groundless.

First of all, Luther was mistaken about the Catholic doctrine of *opus operatum,* for this in no sense limits or replaces faith. Far from putting an emphasis on human activity, it stresses God's activity. This divine action is not conceived of as a miraculous infusion of grace or a magical quality. For the Catholic, every communication of created grace comes about by a personal encounter of God with man. This would indicate that the supposed opposition between a spiritual and ethical justification of the reformed churches and what the evangelical Christian commonly terms Catholic sacramentalism is nothing more than a fiction, a fiction, nevertheless, which played a great part in Luther's break with the Church.

The Catholic doctrine on the Mass can be summarized as follows, using the Catholic concept of *opus operatum.* First of all there is only one sacrifice availing to salvation; the sacrificial death of Our Lord, which took place once and for all on the Cross. The Mass is a re-presentation of this sacrifice. Secondly, the Mass is above all a work of the Lord Himself: He is the priest and the victim. Finally, the priest who celebrates the Mass is an instrument of Christ and a representative of the congregation, of the Mystical Body and a member of this Body. It is difficult to believe that Christians for whom the Gospel is a prime consideration are able to retain traditional prejudices if they recognize that they encounter Our Lord Himself in the mystery of the sacrifice and communion of the Holy Mass, and that Our Lord is there to share with them His cross, His Resurrection, and His Last Supper in a most real manner.

We have ascertained that Luther misunderstood the Catholic doctrine on the Mass to an amazing degree; we must now find out how it was possible for him to be so mistaken on a central point of Catholic doctrine. Luther had been a monk and a priest. How was it possible for his concept of the Mass to be so erroneous?

We must not forget Luther's tendency to exaggerate nor the violence of his invectives against the Mass. Luther's sweeping rejections of Catholic doctrine cannot be easily summarized and presented in strict theological terms. But there is another more important point: the answer to the question we have raised will help us to realize how profound are the causes of the Reformation and how much the Catholic Church must share the responsibility, since Luther's position is quite clearly an answer to a quite deficient understanding of the Mass current in the late medieval period and a piety based univocally on the fruits of the Mass. It is true that this reaction manifested itself after his break with the Church. Current abuses did not seem to play any part in his leaving the Church. After he left the Church, he saw in the approach of many priests to the Mass a confirmation of his position, and more and more frequently they provided the occasion for his unrestrained and quite coarse abuse.

But Luther was not only concerned with externals. Not only did he rage against the lack of reverence, the thoughtlessness and speed with which Mass was said, or the more or less simoniacal selling of good works, but he discovered anew the essentially social character of the Mass in its relation to the Last Supper—a character so well expressed by the term *communion*. The priest, who is ordained not for himself but for the community, should partake of the sacred meal, but so should the faithful as well.

It is not that Luther condemned merely abuses; Luther condemned the Mass itself, because he felt that it was an act of treason to Almighty God. The fact that he was vulnerable to this erroneous interpretation is based ultimately on the nominalistic philosophy that he imbibed during his Catholic period. We have already seen how much of the philosophy of the medieval period resulted in nominalism, as at the University of Paris until its condemnation in 1473 and at a number of the German universities. Nominalistic thought is atomizing, inorganic, and, therefore, peculiarly inept at grappling with the concept of the organic and the sacramental. Starting from nominalistic presuppositions, Luther rejected the Catholic doctrine of the Church and the Mass as the sacrifice of the Church in much the same way that Dr. Eck, one of his principal theological opponents, tried to defend them with the same deficient theological tools.

Other Catholic theologians of the times defended the basic theology of the Mass either in a general way or as the sacrifice of the Mystical Body united under Christ its Head. Catholic theology of the period was not guilty of the massive confusion of the divine and the human as Luther charged.

Our point of departure in this second section is the assertion that certain points of deep opposition between the Catholic and the reformed doctrines are not absolutely irreconcilable. We have considered the example of sacramental priesthood versus universal priesthood. We feel that we have shown that the thesis is tenable. If we consider the whole problem more deeply, keeping our attention on essentials we find that, though the differences are genuine, absolute opposition vanishes.

There is nothing artificial about this procedure. On the contrary, to do so is to be loyal to the truth, since it is capable of a much wider application than we might have suspected. In the antitheses we have mentioned thus far, in Scripture and tradition, individual conscience and the living magisterium, the universal and the sacramental priesthood, the assertion of this second element, which we might term the Catholic, does not eliminate or temper any commitment to the first half of the assertion, which we might call the Evangelical. In fact, each of those elements, Scripture, the universal priesthood, the individual conscience, Catholics seek to affirm as strongly as the Evangelicals. But in Catholic views the second element adds something to the first and takes nothing away. It is important to realize in all these matters that the Catholic assertion of both elements of the antithesis is not an extrinsic attempt to reconcile opposing values. This is a question in fact of a radical unity of the articles of faith in the total complex founded by Jesus that has evolved under the guidance of the Holy Spirit; for example, in Scripture and dogmatic tradition. We are affirming nothing that is against Holy Scripture, because whatever is opposed to Scripture is as uncatholic as it is unevangelical. This does not deny that individual Catholic theologians were a little careless in giving free rein to their logical and deductive tendencies, and thus came dangerously close to formulating a "tradition" that could not be reconciled with Scripture. We are not, however, concerned with individual Catholic theologians but with the common doctrine of the Church that binds all.

There are, of course, other issues on which the Reformation and Catholicism are in absolute contradiction. These are incapable of the type of resolution we have been describing. The extent of opposition is most apparent in the following two areas: the place of man's natural powers in the process of salvation, and the existence of an infallible magisterium. The Reformation rejects both, and to our present day, the opposition between them is insuperable. In both of these matters there is only one approach that offers any hope: it is the answer to the question whether the doctrine of the reformers in this matter is in accordance with Scripture.

The question is whether the Reformation's rejection of the place of man's natural powers in the process of salvation is in accordance with Scripture, or, more exactly, consonant with Scripture as a whole.

The history of the development of the doctrine of the reformers on this point will help us in our search. It would be good to recall some of the conclusions we reached in the second chapter. Luther was a man of distinctive character and temperament; his own experience of sin governed his whole approach to the doctrinal side of the question. He strongly preferred certain parts of Scripture, overemphasizing the Pauline theology of sin and undervaluing what St. James had to say on the subject. From this we concluded that Luther was ill-equipped psychologically to accept Scripture in its totality, that, in fact, he did not so accept Scripture, and that, despite his own wishes in this matter, he was not a docile listener to the whole of the Bible.

We turn now to the Reformation's rejection of the natural powers of man in the process of salvation. I am convinced that the Reformation doctrine is not in accordance with Scripture. There is a vast amount of material at our disposal from which I can choose only a few examples. First, in Genesis 1:31, we find the words: "And God looked upon all that He had made and saw that it was good." Our Lord Himself accepted these words as an expression of the original creative will of God in Matthew 19:4-9. Next we find in the synoptic parables of the servant or the worker in the vineyard not only that the talents and the master's reward are freely given but that the Lord of the vineyard

and the master who gives the talents made a contract with
the servant, demanded a service in return, and recognized
this service. There is nothing that entitles us to omit such
expressions and ideas in our exegesis as though they were
irrelevant. Without doubt, all of our Lord's preaching was
aimed at inner justification and these parables have as their
purpose to show that a mechanical piety that leads a man
to put his trust in his own powers and his own goodness is
false. For this very reason it is especially noteworthy that
Our Lord uses the natural categories of property, reward,
and merit and lets them stand in all their contrast with the
free gift of the Lord and master in his application of the
parable. These considerations are backed up by the fact
that all of Holy Scripture is incessantly appealing to man,
to his good will and cooperation. All of Scripture and especially the New Testament is a summons, a call directed to
man. The New Testament begins with the demand to do
penance: man is to do something; from this point in Scripture man is measured by what he wills to do or not to do.
On this depends his reward or his punishment. Scriptural
texts that speak in this vein are numerous: "If you will enter
eternal life. . . ." (Matt. 19:17); "If you will be perfect,
keep the commandments . . ." (Matt. 19:21); "Whoever
will follow me . . ." (Luke 9:23). Other examples are numerous: Come to me, watch, pray, seek, ask, knock, look,
beware. Consider Matthew: "Thou shalt love the Lord thy
God with thy whole heart and soul and with all thy mind
and strength" (22:37); or, "Then Peter addressed Him,
saying, 'Behold, we have left all and followed thee: what
then shall we have?' And Jesus said to them: 'Amen I say
to you that you who have followed me, in the regeneration
when the Son of Man shall sit on the throne of his glory,
shall also sit on twelve thrones, judging the twelve tribes

of Israel. And everyone who has left house, or brothers, or sisters, or father, or mother, or wife, or children, or lands for my name's sake, shall receive a hundredfold, and shall possess life everlasting'" (19:27).

As Erasmus put it, in all of these parables and appeals we would have to change the workers into idlers if we were to be deaf to these appeals and to deny the repeatedly affirmed connection between the conditions laid down by Our Lord and the success of the work. We'll come back to this point later, but for the moment let's consider John 1:12: "But to as many as received Him he gave the power of becoming sons of God." The whole context illuminates in the most penetrating fashion the complex and mysterious interrelation of God's activity and His call to man; the *Logos* is so overwhelmingly important that man sinks almost to nothingness, but in this text, man's action (receiving Christ) comes before the divine reward. Consider the parable of the talents (Matthew 25:24 ff.). The man is so cautious that he hesitates to use his own talents so that the master won't suffer loss through him. He buries his talent so that he won't lose it, thinking that his master will surely be pleased with his humble estimate of his own abilities, for he shows by this action that he considers himself an unprofitable servant. But the exact opposite happens.

The appeal to man to cooperate with God by good works is expressed with particular force and clarity in the second chapter of the Epistle of St. James. I am not speaking of the reference to faith as dead without good works, but rather of verse 21: "Was not Abraham, our father, justified because of his works?"

The relation of the God who reveals Himself to man is also expressed in the New Testament in the covenant terminology. The whole concept of covenant both in the Old and the New Testament presupposes that God calls upon man to work with Him to achieve some goal and free act of condescension on the part of God, by which God and man become partners, insofar as this expression can be used in connection with God and man.

Note that in all of these remarks I have no intention of isolating man's cooperation, putting it on an independent footing and conceiving of it in a moralistic way. It is obviously totally dependent on the Lord who has given us salvation. When God calls upon man for his response, all depends upon God; He penetrates the entire process of salvation which is entirely enveloped in His grace. But this does not eliminate man's part in the process. How the divine and human rôles are to be reconciled is a mystery, but the impossibility of understanding the mystery cannot touch the fact that each of its elements are true and that Scripture presents each as involving the other.

Another point I would like to emphasize is that, while the texts I have mentioned are all significant in themselves, their real probative power is apparent when they are taken all together. It is then that we realize that we are dealing not with one task of exegesis that might examine a text in isolation from the rest of Scripture and thus tend to derive too much out of merely one text.

Catholic doctrine speaks not only of rewards but also of human merits. Particularly in our own day this seems to be an obstacle for many Evangelical Christians that thus deserves at least a brief comment. If a reward is not given for a meritorious act, for something earned, for something that is mine, the word loses its meaning. The master in the Gospel who speaks so clearly about the reward that the worker will get for his work, expresses this notion with equal clarity in the words: "Take what is yours." But, of

course, the very thing which belongs to the workman is at
the same time the free gift of the master: "And when you
have done all things, say: 'We are unprofitable servants.'"

Furthermore, there are also so-called "superfluous"
merits. This doctrine is by no means an expression of an
arithmetical approach to religion, but quite the opposite; it
is the expression of that very consoling Christian doctrine
of the Communion of Saints. This community or society is
not a pious fiction, but a real and objective fact. It is a community in which all members strengthen one another because they are all of one body, and the life that vivifies all
of the members is the life of Our Lord. When, by virtue of
this life, an individual member is faithful, co-operates with
grace and received a reward for this, this individual member can be a source of strength and a help to others in bear-
ing their burdens.

We do not claim that individual Catholic practice is
always true to this magnificent and consoling doctrine; we
must confess that all too often there is question of merit in
a crude sense, of a mathematical approach to good works
and merits that smacks of moralism and at times of self-
righteousness. When Catholics talk about merit, it would
be a good thing if they would concentrate on affirming the
great truth which they are quite happy to assert in other
connections, that we can merit only by virtue of the grace
of God which is given to us. Think of how prudently and
humbly the liturgy speaks of meriting in the Lord, and I
think that when the word *merit* appears in the liturgy, it
frequently means, "to be made worthy" or "to have the
strength."

We might summarize briefly: In the Protestant attempt
to exalt God by negating the rôle of man, we miss the quality that Peter Lippert has called God's respect for His crea-

ture, His patience, willingness, and desire to wait on His creature's decision. It is a paradoxical thought but at the same time it corresponds perfectly to the fundamental paradox of the preaching of Christ in the New Testament. For this latter reason it would seem to be a good approach for those who find the theological approach of the reformers congenial.

Our general conclusion is that the recognition of the value of the rôle of man in the salvific process is in accordance with Scripture. Furthermore, this recognition is a necessity if revelation and the salvific process are to be taken seriously, and if we are to safeguard the content of revelation as a whole. Conversely, to assert the natural incapacity of man to cooperate in the salvific process is to attack the authenticity of the salvific process itself. For if, as revelation demands, man is to make a response, then that is something which only man can do; if this were impossible for him, God would not have called him to it.

One argument frequently given to substantiate the position of the reformed Churches on this matter asserts that by denying man all part in the salvific process, all of the honor is given to God. He is recognized as the wholly other, the all Holy, and we need never fear exaggeration in giving honor and glory to God; thus in practice we do so by denying man any part in the salvific process. This argument is appealing but false; it originates not in revelation but in human logic and ultimately in the experience of sin, either of man in general or Luther in particular. God has turned to the individual sinner and made His appeal. This means that if God wants me as a partner, then I must believe that I am capable of being His partner. Man does not manifest his greater subjection to the will of God by asserting that he is more powerless than God has willed him to be; objectively, such an attitude is in fact a rejection of the divine will.

The concept of man as a partner of God is not an inadmissible product of confused reasoning. Rather it reaches right to the heart of revelation. To convince ourselves of this and rid our argument of every suggestion that it might be a human though inadequate way of conceiving of the situation, it is enough to meditate on the story of the Annunciation in Luke 1:21-38. It is not simply the story of an announcement. A human interchange occurs in which the Blessed Virgin is asked to give her consent. Only after the angel has calmed her anxiety and answered her questions does she in turn give her reply: "Behold the handmaid of the Lord, be it done unto me according to thy word!" The moment when salvation became a reality was consequent on the agreement of a human being. This is what it means to be a partner of God.

The Catholic concept of the capacity of man to cooperate with God in the salvific process is, of course, shared to a great degree in the understanding and realization of the faith on the part of a number of Evangelical Christians. A glance at the life and prayer of the ministers and members of the Lutheran Church as a whole throughout the past and at present is adequate proof of this. It demonstrates anew that the doctrine of the radical incapacity of man to take part in the salvific process is a task of theology. This in turn gives us good reasons for asking an important question: In Evangelical doctrine on this point do we find a confusion between the reality and a somewhat pedantic theological interpretation of the reality?

This consideration with its possible consequences cannot be rejected on the grounds that it has fastened on an extrinsic addition to the doctrine of the Reformers without an attempt to come to terms with the original Evangelical approach to the problem. The last word certainly hasn't been spoken on Luther's doctrine. Luther's first published work was a moral sermon on the meaning of good works and his constant wavering on the question of man's rôle in salvation has not been sufficiently investigated. Scripture itself, forced him to revise, though not in a systematic way, his original one-sided rejection of any rôle for man in salvation. The Catholic position here is furthered to a significant degree by a large segment of the positive theology of the Reformed Churches, in particular by the increasing number of works that find that Luther gave an incomplete and deficient interpretation of the doctrine of St. Paul and of the Gospel according to St. John because of Luther's reliance solely on the concept of justification. Hermann Mulert puts it well:

It is a question well worth asking whether Luther put such emphasis on the divine omnipotence that few can follow him. What Evangelical Christians, what Lutheran Churches take seriously Luther's principal systematic work "On the Enslaved Will?" ; but if we do not follow the Reformer in this area of prime concern, then our Catholic brethren will quite naturally ask whether the separation between our churches is necessary or was justified.[1]

On the other hand, if Evangelical Christians were to ponder deeply the authentic writings of Catholic saints, I think they would learn soon that Catholics who, by definition, have lived their faith most fully, have not tended to overestimate man's natural abilities but have lived in complete dependence on God, and received from Him the great certitude of their calling.

A second, practically insuperable chasm divides the

[1] *Christliche Welt,* 1930, n. 20.

Churches on the question of a living, infallible teaching power in the Church. In the beginning, the Reformation was directed to a decisive degree against the pope. Today Protestants in general reject the Papacy in much more moderate terms and their rejection itself no longer occupies the place of first importance that it did of old, but the opposition is just as essential as it ever was and nothing has been done to lessen it. This is another area where the defenders of the Catholic position can only strive to show that their rejection of the position of the reformers is justified.

Even more clearly than in the question of man's rôle in the salvific process, we meet in this controversy all of the essential problems involved in interconfessional dialog. In it we come to the limits that can be reached in discussion. Here, even less than in other matters, all of us, Evangelical as well as Catholic Christians, cannot hope to clarify all the issues and bridge the chasm which separates us, with any rapidity. The reason is that the point under discussion is just one manifestation of two completely different ways of looking at things, which, in turn, permit or render difficult or impossible a given interpretation of a certain part of Scripture. We are dealing here with two different ways of understanding the New Testament, with two different ways of reading Scripture. It will be much to the point to say a few words about the justification of these two positions.

It will be profitable to recall that the Catholic theses or other similar ones concerning the nature of the primitive Christian community have grown continually in their acceptance, especially since modern historical and exegetical criticism have freed themselves on the one hand from the dominance of idealism and pseudo-scientific relativism and their stubborn anti-Catholic prejudices on the other. (Adolf

Harnack's work is quite symbolic here.) Fifty or sixty years ago such a rapprochment would have seemed impossible to serious students. Yet it would seem probable now that further scientific studies may bring Catholics and Protestants into closer agreement on this point.

Much contemporary Evangelical theology is also quite close to Catholic theology on another fundamental point: the assertion that Christianity was not preached by Our Lord as a formless doctrine, but was concretized in an actual Church, founded by Christ, and that the very first Christian generation already possessed a faith whose structure was complete in all its essentials, one in which there was a real hierarchy. When Peter and Paul claimed the right to speak authoritatively at the First Council of Jerusalem, to determine the correct doctrine, then we cannot assert that a teaching office that is given the authority to decide binding doctrine is irreconcilable with the Church as Jesus founded it, or that the doctrine of an infallible teaching authority is in contradiction with the New Testament.

Among the more general elements involved in the discussion of an infallible teaching authority is the question of Tradition in the Church. By Tradition we do not mean a development brought about by chance occurrences of history, but rather the expression of the essence of the Church that is protected by the Holy Ghost—the Church against which the gates of hell shall not prevail. It would seem possible for a very profound understanding to take place here as well. If the Reformation asserts that revelation closed with the death of the last Apostle in such a manner that a vital development of the foundation laid by the Founder would be impossible, and that revelation is contained exclusively and completely in the written word of

the Bible, it would seem to be making something artificial
and unnatural out of the living structure of the Church. It
seems to strip the parable of the grain of mustard seed of
most of its meaning. To do this would be to reject an obvious development in the apostolic Church.

Here we encounter another obstacle in the way of understanding. The Reformation interrupted the vital stream
of tradition; in many respects it represented a new and autonomous beginning. The Reformed Churches spoke a new
language; they strove with all their might to go back over
the fourteen centuries that separated them from the first
Christian generation. Could they succeed? The Reformed
Churches separated themselves from Tradition. One of the
great achievements of modern science has been to labori-
ously reconstruct a great number of individual details,
which, at least on the practical level, the Catholic Middle
Ages were neither aware of nor possessed. Yet history is
not the same as Tradition, for the whole is more than the
sum of all its parts. When history has spoken, we still must
adhere to a living tradition. No matter how Evangelical
Christians wish to judge the scope of the apostolic tradition
preserved in the Catholic Church, the fact cannot be denied
that its teaching authority, prayer, and asceticism have
maintained a close contact with this tradition.

There is one more critically important point: the Reformation was a return to the Bible alone, i.e., to a previously known and well determined collection of holy books
of the Old and the New Testament. The Reformers asserted
along with the Catholics that these books and these alone
contained the inspired word of God. How do they know?
The Bible itself makes this assertion to merely a limited degree, and its testimony is almost wholly wanting in regard
to the entire New Testament. The Reformers accepted this

judgment from the Church, the Church from which they got the Bible itself. In so doing, the Reformation is not true to its cardinal principle, the rejection of dogmatic tradition, because that which it regards as its own deepest foundation rests precisely on dogmatic tradition.

Now we come to the question of the infallible teaching authority. The decisive point here is the primacy of Peter, a foundation laid in the New Testament itself for the infallible teaching authority of the Church. Here the critical text is Matthew 16:18, Our Lord's answer to the confession Peter had just made through an inspiration from heaven, "And I say to thee, thou art Peter, and upon this rock I will build my Church, and the gates of hell shall not prevail against it."

Critical exegesis of the present commonly recognizes Peter's primacy in the original Christian community; today, practically no one tries to limit the extent of the promise made to Peter by questioning the authenticity of the text.

In the second and third parts of Our Lord's answer to Peter, the future tense is used, and it would seem that we do not do justice to this if we allow the Church to stand on a rock-solid foundation only for the duration of Peter's life. Furthermore, the connection with the final part, dealing with the resistance of the Church to the gates of hell, is clear. It surely can't mean that the powers of hell will be contained only during the lifetime of Peter. If Our Lord founded a Church which was to last until the end of the world, then the assurance he gave to Peter must be valid for all time.

A further point is that the Church never restricted its understanding of Our Lord's promise to apostolic times. It developed the papal primacy from the beginning which all Christians recognized and accepted until the time of the

Reformation. Neither the Reformation itself nor the Reformed Churches today are sufficiently conscious of the
frightful implications of this fact, if, as is said, the primacy
of the pope is the manifestation of the Antichrist and a
realization of an essentially unchristian fact. The Lord
promised that the Holy Spirit would stand by His Church
and lead it to all truth. If the thesis of the reformers is correct, then from the end of the first century, or at least from
the third or fourth century, the Church was in error and
remained in error for a millenium. This would make in
fact the entire history of the Church one of error and
heresy—a frightening and theologically impossible conclusion.

I strongly believe that our Evangelical brethren should
consider this point deeply. Here we are faced with an absolute choice. Luther's frightful invective must be carried
to its logical conclusion: either the Papacy was founded by
Our Lord or it is truly the Antichrist; there are no half-
way reconciliations possible for the Papacy.

In passing I would like to call attention to the fact that
the primacy texts of the New Testament were written at a
time when there existed no practical need for a primacy,
nor, humanly speaking, the possibility of conceiving of it.
Not only is the content of the text reassuring; so is the
strong contrast of the text with the historical situation in
which it was written and spoken.

We can also approach the question very fruitfully from
the standpoint of church history, i.e., from the modern developments of the principles laid down by the reformers.

I already noted that in the formal concept of Christianity, as doctrine and dogma, Luther was in agreement
with the Roman Church and both were in agreement with
the Gospel. The Catholic Church has continued to teach

that Christianity is essentially and unconditionally characterized by such dogmatic teachings. In the course of the
centuries, however, Luther's concept has been abandoned
by ever-increasing numbers in the Evangelical Churches to
a degree that has involved the rejection of the fundamental
principles of the original reformers. Within the different
Evangelical Churches there has occurred to a significant
degree a practical as well as theoretical rejection of ecclesiastical authority. For a number of Evangelical Christians
this has come to mean a denial of most of the articles of the
Christian faith. Such a compromise with relativism contrasts most sharply with the Catholic position that has always
been characterized by unyielding dogmatic intolerance.

It is true that in the battles of the Reformation itself,
and in the interconfessional strife of succeeding years, this
dogmatic intolerance frequently prevented Catholics from
fully understanding the issues of the Reformation. We cannot guess what might have happened if Catholic firmness
in matters of doctrine had been joined with the ability to
perceive a Catholic heritage in the Reformation. Undoubtedly men would have failed to assert the truth with charity.
Dogmatic intolerance was an absolute necessity. The later
history of Protestantism is evidence that the caution manifest by Catholics in this matter was justified.

Furthermore, history gives facts to show how the Catholic Church can claim that she has defended certain important principles and doctrines of the Reformation
through her dogmatic intolerance so that the Church is
heir of these points of Christian doctrine, more than a considerable part, even the majority, of the Evangelical denominations.

This is the most important thesis. The decisive point, if
our discussions are to bear fruit, is: Is the later Protestant

rejection of the principles of the Reformation a necessary consequence of these principles themselves? This question we will examine now. Since it is of the deepest existential significance for Evangelical Christians, we must proceed with the greatest sincerity and tact. Before I go any further, I would like to ask the Protestant reader to recall the spirit in which we are discussing all these questions. In a mutual search we are dedicated to strive for the truth in love. Our great concern must be to eliminate a tendency to judge one another unfavorably, a sense of superiority, and especially a rejoicing over a weakness of another's position.

The ultimate rejection of the principles of the Reformation followed as a logical consequence of the rejection of an infallible teaching authority in the Church. This assertion can be proven both historically and theoretically. Both methods of proof shed light upon one another.

The course of the Reformation movement itself is identical to an historical proof. After Luther, the major figures of the Reformation were Karlstadt, Zwingli, and Munzer. Their interpretation of Christianity was founded on the same formal principle as that Luther claimed to use: personal interpretation of Holy Scripture according to one's own conscience. The outcome was a difference of opinions that came to full contradiction in essential matters of doctrine. Luther recognized and affirmed this fact in his sentences of condemnation against the visionaries and Zwingli. Lutheran theology and in fact Evangelical theology as a whole has been too prone to regard this opposition as a matter of course, whereas it is actually a serious charge against Evangelical principles as such. As Heiler has correctly observed, no more serious criticism can be levelled at Luther's whole approach and at the fundamental principles of the Reformation in general than this contradictory juxtaposition of Lutheran, Reformed, Evangelical, and Protestant interpretations of *one* Christianity.

These divisive tendencies manifested themselves in many ways from the first decade of the Reformation and have been operative throughout the whole history of Reform Christianity. In fact the process of division was continuous while rejections on the doctrinal plane became more radical as time went on. With a man such as Jacob Accontius the Enlightenment had to a great extent already begun in the sixteenth century. Even the significant movements of inner renewal in the following centuries (Pietism, for example) continued of their own inner necessity to erode the objective content of the revealed doctrine. We are well aware of the tragic effects of this process of erosion during the eighteenth, nineteenth, and twentieth centuries.

The results are well known but no less terrible for that reason. We are faced with a Christianity hopelessly divided that adds to the confusion by teaching a great number of opposing doctrines. Not only do we see that an astonishingly high percentage of Protestants of all confessions deny the truth of fundamental articles of the Christian faith, but worst of all they have to a great extent lost the sense that Christianity is a genuine revelation, that truth is unique, and must remain so. In this mortal sickness we can find the reason for the failure of Christianity to speak convincingly to the men of our age.

In the gradual development of the Reformation a rejection of fundamental ideas and the eventual rejection of its own starting point can be grasped without too much difficulty. The doctrines of the Reformation were essentially an absolute affirmation of one aspect of a complex reality. As such, they tended toward an exaggerated view. Every one-sided approach eventually comes to the point where it rejects its own starting point. Extreme positions are really quite close to each other. Just as the inner logic of fideism developed into rationalism or hypercriticism, so the Reformation, in rejecting any true development within Christianity, explained the tradition of the preceding centuries as a merely human phenomenon. Consequently, the Reformed Churches became vulnerable to an increasing degree of being explained as stages in a process of evolution; the very foundations of the reform faith came to be merely regarded as human. As such they were criticized and attacked and rejected as merely human. The concept of revelation, inspiration, of the divinity of Christ, and so on, were sacrificed to a hypercriticism that grew directly from reformed theology (although we must not forget the corrosive elements of the theology of pre-reformation days and the harm caused by philosophy in the period following.)

The objection is sometimes raised that an infallible teaching authority is not justified because it is very useful. From an examination of the historical consequences of the Reformation I have not proven that the Papacy was a very useful arrangement. Rather the history of the Reformed Churches and denominations is a striking proof that for the preservation of Christian truth an infallible teaching authority is an absolute necessity. If the possibility of error is a grave but necessary concern, and if we are going to engage in the search for truth, this too—I mean objectively but not as a reproach—is a half-truth and an expression of compromise with modern relativism. The only reply is to ask which is more important, an open wound that can cause death and most certainly will, or life itself. We are dealing with a matter which threatens the life of Christianity. The entire primitive Church knew nothing of this threat. Can we say that within the Evangelical congregations we encounter a continual process of renewal? I would not want to do anything to minimize the least sign of inner renewal in the Protestant Churches, because the more we find, the better it is for all Christianity and the easier the task of all Christians. Yet, if we look at the situation honestly, can we discern an inner renewal that has gotten to the heart of the matter to any notable degree? Do we find renewal today in dialectical theology and the renaissance of Lutheranism? We do. For this we can thank God, since it has made possible our interconfessional dialogue. Although we have much to rejoice over in this vital new movement, nevertheless, we must recognize that the revival of concern for revelation touches only a small segment of the Protestant community with almost no effect on the largely secular ethical climate that passes itself off as Christian. Remember too that we have no guarantee that this new understanding of faith, revelation, and the divine element in Christianity that has been achieved by a segment of Evangelical Christendom will survive the attacks of the rationalists and demythologizers. The reason is that Evangelical Christianity has no objective method to lay permanent claim to these new achievements. For now, as always, the interpretation of revelation rests ultimately on the conscience of the individual. No statement or creed of an Evangelical Church can bind the individual Christian.

The essential proof for the necessity of doctrinal divisions consequent upon the rejection of an infallible teaching authority is based on the ambiguity of human speech. Scripture itself bears witness to this ambiguity in the account of the second temptation of Our Lord, in Matthew 4:5. We can make absolutely clear statements only in the realm of the simplest mathematical statements. All statements dealing with the meta-empirical order are more or

less ambivalent, and the more profound and embracing
they are, the greater the ambivalence. Certainty of the exact
meaning in individual cases depends on an appeal to a
living interpretation; in our case, only if we can turn to an
infallible teaching authority as a last resort. No matter how
much we try to exclude our personal prejudices, no matter how honorable our intentions to hear only the Word
of God, if left to ourselves, we not only find the many-
faceted riches of Scripture but also are led to affirm contradictory teachings. The whole history of philosophy and
religion, of Christian heresies, and finally of the Reformation itself, is convincing proof of a statement that Luther
himself affirmed in his First Lecture on the Psalms: "Unless doctrine is authoritatively promulgated by a living
human being endowed with the authority to teach, there
will be as many doctrines as there are heads."

We can now summarize our statements of the limits
which Catholics must put on their agreement with the
fundamental issues of the Reformation. Although some opposing opinions may be capable of resolution, the Catholic
rejection of other and more essential issues and ideas of the
Reformation has strong scriptural and historical support.
Although in many respects Catholics must limit, in essentials, their agreement with the fundamental doctrines of the
Reformers, in other and equally essential matters Catholics
share the concerns of the Evangelical and Reformed
Churches.

We come now to the last part of our discussions: to
what extent does the Catholic Church, as it actually exists
today, correspond to the claims which we made in her
name. We cannot cover every facet of this complex picture, so we will choose just one point which can serve as a
particularly fruitful one for a religious and theological en-

counter: the coming of age of the laity in the Church, the realization of the universal priesthood and of the freedom of the individual Christian. Surely all of these are central concerns of Evangelical Christians.

Since the eleventh century, to an increasing degree, the Catholic Church in the West became a Church of the clergy and, at times, a Church of clericalism. This clericalism has been able to survive into modern times, after the Reformation and the Council of Trent. It often survived in the lamentable forms of the *ancien régime*—the clergy constituted a legally, socially, and economically privileged class. The clergy were the masters in the Church; too often the laity were merely those on whom the mastery was exercised. Even today we find traces of this clericalism in the Church, because many are not sufficiently concerned and unyielding in their efforts to realize the basic principle formulated by Pope Pius X, the very Pope who started preparations for the new Code of Canon Law: *salus populi, suprema lex:* the highest law is the salvation of the people. The principal concern is not the rights of priests and pastors but the pastoral needs of the people. We are not fully aware of the fact that every Catholic has the right and the duty to ask questions and to offer his advice and his entreaties to the administrators of the Church.

It is true that here and there, not excluding the Roman Curia, there is the danger that fruitful cooperation can turn into deadly uniformity in which formalizing and centralizing elements predominate. A further danger exists that many of the externals of Church administration may come to be regarded as absolutes, in practice or through a false belief that developments which are actually quite new once were part of the Church in earlier times. Another danger rests in looking only at the fact that we are secure in our faith, without being aware that no matter how secure we are in our faith, faith still involves the taking of a risk. Faith is a commitment which must color the whole of our Christian lives. We might also ask whether the profound saying of Our Lord about the weeds growing with the wheat until the harvest time (Matt. 13:29) has been truly understood. It is, after all, the deep insight of God Himself into the laws of growth of spiritual life and the insight of the masterful Teacher Himself into the psychic damage that can be done by an inopportune interference with these same laws of growth. We must also admit that there is too much fear about giving lay people in the Church real responsibility; there is the feeling abroad that this might not be in the best interests of the Church. I could add much more that would be quite discouraging, and if I were addressing Catholics alone, I would do so, and not behind closed doors. For if there is one thing we need, it is fresh air in these areas.

It is healthy to know that you are being observed and judged from outside your own fold. Throughout the history of the Church, her great men had no hesitation in publicly confessing and condemning the abuses whether they existed among priests, bishops, or the Holy See. Of course, this was done contritely with loyalty and charity. Merely recall that Augustine made the story of his great sins a part of world literature and did so without petty anxiety or the desire to minimize. St. Bernard spoke quite clearly about the abuses at the Roman court. Thomas of Celano in his first "Life of St. Francis," whom he admired so much, had no hesitation in affirming that, before his conversion, the Saint had lived a worse life than even his parents had." The statement of our Lord, "Get thee behind me, Satan," to Peter the Rock of the Church, as well as the account of Peter's pit-

iable weakness on the night of the Passion or even after
the coming of the Holy Spirit at Antioch, have, under the
inspiration of the same Holy Spirit, been recorded in the
New Testament where they are to be proclaimed to the
world.

Many, likewise, are quite surprised at the strange, in-
visible wall that has grown up between the clergy and the
Catholic people. I am not speaking here primarily of the
opposition we sometimes see between the laity, especially
the better educated ones, and the clergy. Though in connection with this I would like to remark that, no matter
what the justification of such opposition is, it is a disquieting fact which forces us to ask important questions; this is
a good thing. But to get back to the point: well-meaning
and dedicated priests often find that they fail to reach a
deep understanding of the problems of the lay people of
today, whether the particular laity involved are cultured or
not. Unfortunately a number of priests are content to remain in their spiritually and economically secure world, a
closed world, one effectually isolated from reality. I think
that the circumstances of this final lecture preclude any
necessity of my assuring you that there are other members
of the clergy who are completely different as an over-cau-
tious apologetics would demand.

I know that none of my listeners will be surprised that,
after warning the clergy of certain defects in their attitude
toward the laity, I turn toward the laity to remind them of
their strict duty to preserve their loyalty to the Church and
to strive with all their power to eliminate from the Church
types of clericalism we have described no matter what sacrifices are involved. No man can sulk in his tent or confine
his criticism to members of his own circle and still claim to
be Christian provided his criticism is justified. Within the

Church we all have a duty to serve. This means that a vast amount of work lies before us if the laity are going to assume their rightful place in the life of the Church.

But there is another aspect of the picture, and today a most important one. Presently we are at a turning point in the life of the Church. If I am right and if the laity and clergy live up to their responsibilities, the coming age will be the age of the laity—in the Church, with the Church, and for the Church. The laity will work in full accord with, and in subordination to, the teaching authority of the Church but will remain the dominant element in the history of the Church.

This deserves some explanation. We are assuming that whatever is summarized in the term, *clericalism*, concerns merely the practical order and not the basic structure of the Church. Yet the elements I see operative in this critical period of the Church are not all peripheral and unessential at the present time. On the contrary they are the realization of fundamental Catholic doctrines that have never been entirely forgotten, for the essential participation of the laity in the life of the Church is based on the reality of the new life given to each baptized person.

In our day the proper areas of responsibility and mature participation in the life of the Church by the laity are being recognized and even demanded in significant areas of Church life. I do not base this assertion on a number of encouraging individual steps that have been taken, because often enough we see the phenomenon of one step forward, two steps backward. Rather I think that we should ground our hope in the fact that the new rôle of the laity springs from a movement of reform whose foundations are wide and deep—specifically, a realization of the *metanoia* that is spoken of in the New Testament, and from the emphasis on the value of true internal sanctity. The indications of the new rôle of the laity are more indicative of things to come insofar as they resemble the truth spoken in Scripture: "He said this not of himself but because he was high priest of that year" (John 11:51). All of these movements correspond to the needs and demands of our day and coincide with the elimination of the last elements of the medieval world that were effective in forming the clericalism we have mentioned. They coincide with the progress of the masses throughout the world. All of these movements have a deep inner unity. At times this is not too apparent because their points of departure are so diverse, flowing from different pastoral problems. Only a superficial and inexperienced judge would find in these movements an example of clever, calculated, and comprehensive planning on the part of the Roman authorities. The true secret of their vitality is that they arise from a profound Christian inspiration that is always striving to embody the heart of the Christian ideal. All of these movements of their own inner necessity involve the laity, the special element in the Church's organism that is most patiently waiting for an awakening and one that is fully capable of understanding and penetrating the modern world, the rechristianization of which has been the main concern of the Church since the time of Leo XIII.

Since you are well acquainted with these movements, a few indications will suffice. These are linked to three of the greatest Popes of recent times, Pius X, Pius XI, and Pius XII, individually and collectively to be numbered gifts of God to His Church and to the whole world.

I know that when I mention Pius X in this group, a number of my Protestant listeners will have definite reservation, because they have been given an inadequate picture of this Pope. Particular, unfortunately phrased sections of the *Encyclical on Charles Borromeo* have been repeated over and over. But of course, we cannot understand Pius X through this Encyclical, still less through a few excerpts from it. In the final analysis, he was only formally responsible for it. Neither are the inadequacies of the necessary fight against Modernism adapted to recognize the tremendous significance of this dedicated supreme pastor. Pius' character is revealed most clearly in the liturgical movement which he started and which has grown so rapidly. The liturgical movement means nothing less than the active participation of the laity in the essential prayer and sacrifice of the Church, as is stated quite explicitly in the Encyclical *Mystici corporis* of Pope Pius XII.

The liturgical movement has as its purpose the deepening of Christian existence, an emphasis on the substantial elements of Christian life and the relegation of the peripheral elements to their proper place. The Eucharist, the altar, our common sacrifice, and our common sacrificial meal—these are the sources of our unity.

Think of the contributions of Pius XI. The canonization of St. Joan of Arc by his predecessor, Benedict XV, and his own canonization of St. Thomas More mean more than an increase of two more in the official list of Saints. In these two Saints a new element joins the almost infinite varieties of sanctity possible in the Church. Particularly appealing in our own day, it frees the Catholic concept of sanctity from certain unauthentic elements which have caused much misunderstanding both within and outside of the Church. In both Saints we have the ideal of lay-sanctity manifest in fully human form.

Let us consider Thomas More first. His life, work, and

writings were of great significance before his canonization. Now he is placed before us as a Saint in all of his completely human grandeur and good sense. Fortunately we have Holbein's portrait of Thomas More so that no one can say that he went around with his head piously tilted, radiating dedication and perpetual rapture. He does not fit into the categories of the ordinary and expected appearance of saints. Here we have a true human being, a gifted humanist, a leading statesman of his day, dedicated father and a man who exemplified the finest in the culture of his times.

The most profound meaning in both of these canonizations is that they represent the canonization of the Christian conscience, particularly so in the case of St. Joan of Arc who obeyed her conscience and the "voices" she heard in opposition to an ecclesiastical court.

Returning to the works of Pope Pius XII, his founding of Catholic Action, far from being a movement with a mere slogan, was a divinely inspired designation of a movement which has awakened powerful sources of revival. As the Pope himself explained, Catholic Action is the participation of the laity in the apostolate of the hierarchy. These words can be repeated so often that they lose their meaning for us, but in themselves they have a profound meaning that penetrates to the heart of the pastoral needs and possibilities of today. A number of priests and prelates, quite cautious about the notion of Catholic Action, seem to relegate it to the class of one more harmless activity among others. Nevertheless the statement of the Pope remains and, as it might be seen from the results in France, Catholic Action can become quite fruitful.

Another aspect of Pius XI's pontificate was his rather daring affirmation of the national elements of the Church in the missions of Japan, Manchuria, and later in China. Decisions made, whose effect is to herald the downfall of clericalism, cannot be properly evaluated for a long time.

Next we have the biblical movement which has brought about a gradual penetration of the Word of God into theology, preaching, and the religious life of the Church to an extent more profound than any since the beginning of the Middle Ages. No matter what reservations must be made, this phenomenon can be explained only through the mysterious power of the Word written by God Himself and spoken by Jesus Christ. It involves a way of thinking, praying, and theologizing that is based on the New Testament and of necessity makes great areas of traditional Catholic doctrine available once more. The prophecy made by Bishop Besson of Fribourg may come true: "Our Fathers split over the Word of God, but it is through the Word of God that we will come together once more." In this regard, if Catholic and Protestant scholars can produce a text of the Bible that receives the approval of the Church, then we will have a great bond of unity.

We must evaluate all these movements not only in themselves, but also in terms of a significant and quite general transformation among the faithful concerning their relation to the Church. Guardini noted this important development back in the 1920's and called it the awakening of the Church in the souls of the faithful.

We are not inclined today to indulge in a somewhat carefree optimism of those times. We are aware that from human and Christian aspects we are weak and powerless to overcome the split of five hundred years' duration in a day, particularly through mere theories or activist programs. At the same time, however, we may hope that the beginnings we have noted will develop. Pastoral needs, above all the preaching of the Word, will make this development a necessity and do much to bring about a mature laity in the Church. Perhaps this will be sooner than we would expect. If so, it will make evident the extent to which Christian existence as such is threatened.

The movements that we discussed show that our concept of the Church, of prayer and preaching, have taken on a coloring that appears quite congenial to Evangelical Christians. Our use of such terms as "universal priesthood," "the freedom of the Christian," etc., is quite familiar to them; yet we use them now because the life of the Church in our day is *more* Catholic than before. There is no question of innovation but rather of profound renewal. Newman had the key word for all of this: *realization*.

I know that Protestants will have certain reservations about the picture I have drawn. It gives the appearance of being made to order for Protestants, of having little to do with the daily routine of the ordinary Catholic parish. These reservations are quite understandable. They depend on elements operative in the era preceding the Reformation and in the Reformation itself. As a reaction to Catholic attitudes manifest in the struggle against the Reformation and the Reformed Churches right up to our own days, they are in part based on impressions made by peripheral elements of ordinary Catholic practice. Now of all people, we should be the last to depict the concrete situation as though it did justice to the ideal. Nevertheless, these reservations are not really justified; these usually flow from a deficient understanding of the Church that was common in the days when Protestants and Catholics faced one another as hostile forces. For instance, time and time again, we find Protestants asserting that Catholics cannot follow their individual consciences or, at the very least, the Catholic is too often subject to the interference of the teaching authority of the Church. The answer is that Catholics do take the Church seriously. We confess that we are not the ultimate authorities in interpreting the message of Christ, that we must receive it from the Church, and that we have to form our consciences as members of the Church. But it is still true that for the Catholic as for other Christians, his conscience is the court of last resort; whatever goes against the dictates of conscience is a sin.

Another element stands in the way of Protestant confidence and understanding of the Church which is quite often painful to Catholics as well. It is the slow tempo of change in the Church, particularly in the Catholic renewal of which we have been talking, a seeming hesitation in getting rid of some of the formalism and externalism that mar the Church. Reform measures are proposed with good will and sincere dedication. Yet they meet with resistance. In this matter, history confirms what a careful consideration of the facts would indicate: a violent interruption in the process of growth can be avoided only if the rate of development is slow. This slow rate of growth is the best guarantee that the harvest will be as great as this is possible on this earth, as Newman pointed out so well.

Actually this slow rate of change in the Church exemplifies the basic law of Christianity that those who follow Luther in his theology of the Cross should understand well. For the Church's slow tempo is a particular form of carrying the Cross for those who have come to see the pressing need of a real renovation in the Church. Here again we must realize that in Christianity it is not the way a man sees things as an individual that counts but the way he sees them in union with the whole Church that is led by the Holy Ghost. Remember, too, that one man sows while another reaps. Remember, above all, that much more important than our own individual insights is our sincerity in affirming "Thy will be done"—an affirmation which we make most authentically when we have every reason in the world for saying no. In this way, through sacrifice imposed from without, a man can be brought little by little to grasp the paradoxical power of anonymous obedience, a factor in the history of the Church about which little has been said.

We should say a word about the frequently mentioned opposition to things Roman as such. This played an important rôle during the Reformation period, sometimes with good reason, sometimes without, but without doubt from the Counter Reformation and later periods we could produce much material to substantiate opposition. This does not concern us now. Our concern is with the present and it is disturbing to see how widespread anti-Roman feeling is in the Protestant Churches today, especially a widespread feeling that deceitful political maneuvering is the only concern of the Curia.

I know that my readers will not feel that out of a mistaken love for my Church I am distorting the picture. Yet I must point out that the documents which have fostered and promoted the movements in the Church of which I have spoken are not political, but essentially religious documents. These make stern demands on the members of the Church but are at the same time priceless expressions of the Church's love for her children. They indicate the religious concern of official Catholic circles. Far from being polemic in intent, they are efforts to realize the fullness of our Christian faith, to realize the evangelical ideal in the Church. As such they merit trust and confidence.

We are not living in the days of the Renaissance popes

or the days of the *ancien regime*. The extravagant enthusiasm which many Catholics used to manifest for all things
connected with the Vatican during past decades is fortunately a thing of the past. Yet, precisely for this reason, we
are in a position to indulge in some restrained enthusiasm
without fearing that someone may say, "he doth protest too
much." We do not have any need to examine all of the
writings of Pope Pius XII in an attempt to reduce all of the
addresses of this incredibly active Pope to a common denominator in order to be deeply moved by the significance
of his religious concerns. His address at the World Eucharistic Congress in Budapest in 1938 is one without parallel
in the entire history of the Church; profoundly moving,
prayerful, deeply liturgical, his appeal was based on the
very core ideas of the Christian revelation.

In his Christmas message of 1943 to the Cardinals the
same Pope proclaimed that for the period of suffering of
that time there was need to confront the great task which
faced the Church without prejudice and with joy and the
courage of strong hearts, "who are prepared to assist at
the renewal of the mystery of the Cross." A noted German
Lutheran for more than six decades, Baron von Pechmann
of Munich, said of his first encyclical, "Here we have not
only the voice of the honored head of the Roman Catholic
Church; here we have the Holy Spirit Himself, the one,
holy, Christian Church, speaking through the mouth of a
dedicated man."

It is time now to sum up and draw our conclusions.
First of all, the "exclusive formulas" which characterized
Protestantism, such as *sola fides sola Scriptura*, etc., are
still in opposition to the "inclusive formulas" which char-
acterize Catholicism, such as faith and works, Scripture
and Tradition, etc. The opposition that still persists is not

insuperable in principle; both series of formulas reflect a common Christian concern. The struggle to regain our appreciation of this common Christian concern after four hundred years is not an attempt to suppress or hush up these points of opposition. It is merely the first step—and an important one. If it is followed up, then the day will come when the gap can be bridged. I think that this is particularly true of our concern to help our Protestant brethren become aware of some points in the Gospel which they have become accustomed to skip over in their reading for so long a time.

In closing, I would like to recall to the mind of the reader that it has been my concern that Protestants and Catholics realize that our discussions in common must be of profound, existential concern to all of us. Now that we have covered so much ground together, we can never look on one another as we did before. We are all aware of our responsibility for the future of Christianity. We took as our point of departure the imminent dechristianization of the West. We saw that we are confronted with just two possibilities: either the West will become Christian again, or it will be destroyed. We recognized that the dechristianization of the West is to a great extent conditioned by the split within Christendom. This is the source of inner weakness, and especially of a lessening of the convincing power of the Christian message to affect the non-Christian world. Thus a rechristianization of the West and thereby of the world involves in essence the unity of Christendom. In view of this, if we truly deserve the name of Christians, we must make our own the concerns of the great high-priestly prayer of Our Lord: "that they all may be one."

Now this concern is going to make important demands upon us, which I would like to express in the words of two men deeply involved in the question of religious union: Cardinal Newman and Professor Rademacher of Bonn. It was Cardinal Newman who said, "We are all guilty, those of us who left the Church as well as those of us who remained within the Church; we all need conversion. The individual Catholic and the Catholic community must return to the fullness of Catholic truth and the full realization of the Catholic idea just as much as anyone else." It was Rademacher who said, "Religious and ecclesiastical unity can come about only if we are willing to go to meet our separated brethren, to listen to what they have to say, to be willing to learn from them." We must remember that when religious unity does come, it will be a new Pentecost, a free gift of the Holy Spirit. All we can do is strive to make ourselves ready, and the beginning and end of our preparations must be our striving to be authentically Christian, to live more fully the new life which our common Lord Jesus Christ has given us and to become more deeply rooted in Him. It is our duty to pray for this unity in the spirit of the high-priestly prayer of Our Lord.

Is it really asking too much of our faith, my fellow Christians, if we hope that these words of Our Lord on the subject of unity will, if we take them to heart, allow us no rest until we have done our best to prepare the way. These words will quiet our faint-hearted objections and help us to say with the fulness of faith, in the spirit of asking for a new Pentecost for the Church, "Come, Lord Jesus!"

Let us all, Protestant and Catholic Christians, pray the high-priestly prayer of Our Lord:

Yet not for these only do I pray, but for those also who through their word are to believe in me, that all may be one, even as thou, Father, in me and I in thee; that they also may be one in us, that the world may believe that thou hast sent me. And the glory that thou hast given me I have given to them, that they may be one just as we are one: I in them and thou in me; that they may be perfected in unity and that the world may know that thou hast sent me, and that thou hast loved them even as thou hast loved me.

Father, I will that where I am, they also whom thou hast given me may be with me; in order that they may behold my glory which thou hast given me, because thou hast loved me before the creation of the world. Just Father, the world has not known thee, but I have known thee, and these have known that thou hast sent me. And I have made known to them thy name and will make it known in order that the love with which thou hast loved me may be in them and I in them (John 17:20-26).

"I am confident that He who has begun a good work in you will bring it to perfection" (Phil 1:6).

A NOTE ON THE TYPE

IN WHICH THIS BOOK IS SET

This book is set in Times Roman, a Linotype face created by Stanley Morrison, world-famous typographical authority. It was designed for the London *Times,* which demanded a type face that should be clear and legible, precise but not mechanical, having a high letter but not condensed, of a "color" suitable for any paper or printing process, with character but not with annoying characteristics. The clear, open characters of Times Roman are the secret of its clear printing on any paper, whether it be on the coarsest of newsprint or the finest coated paper. This book was composed and printed by the Wickersham Printing Company of Lancaster, Pa., and bound by Moore and Company of Baltimore. The typography and design are by Howard N. King.